Table of Contents

Introduction

"Emotional Intelligence is a master aptitude, a capacity that profoundly affects all other abilities, either facilitating or interfering with them"
Daniel Goleman
Author

Two and a half years ago I visited a school that ran a programme in social and emotional learning. It was a sharp and invigorating November day; I decided to enjoy the journey, take the underground and walk. Eventually I found the school, having asked the way from the usual array of second-hand-car salesmen, small groups walking in the neighbourhood park, and the local police. I was a bit taken aback to be met by two imposing, armed security guards at the school gates. They seemed something of a paradox for a school that was determined to make an impact on the social and emotional learning of its students, and gave me a moment of reflection about my recent casual stroll.

I had an appointment with the leader of the school's programme, Sandy Parker. Dedicated and tirelessly committed to the development of learning for young people, she had a hard-nosed grasp of the challenges that confront them today. She was confident in her belief that the work they were doing at the school would make a difference for all young people, some of whom were otherwise destined to fail in school as well as in life.

Sandy knew the problems her students brought to school and she knew she couldn't make them disappear. She couldn't remove the poverty, mend the broken homes, remove the alcohol and drug abuse or turn every experience a child had in school into a magical event of learning. What she did believe was that she could help her students look at their world in a different way. That she could show them how to overcome the sense of helplessness, how to value themselves, develop lasting relationships, learn from conflict rather than be a martyr to it and be a success both in the classroom and in their lives. She believed that she could show young people how they learn and help them take away those self-inflicted blocks to learning that deprive so many young people of access to this most fabulous of all human activities.

"What lies before us and what lies behind us are small matters compared to what lies within us. And when we bring what is within out into the world, miracles happen"

Henry Thoreau 1817–62
Author and Naturalist

The school had a strong belief in its students' ability to learn; a belief that the achievement of the students represented only a fraction of their potential. A belief that all students are intrinsically motivated to learn, but too often cut themselves off from the key that will unlock fabulous achievement, success, enjoyment and personal fulfilment. The school's goal was to engage the motivation that young people have to learn, take away those self-inflicted inhibitions to learning, develop positive beliefs about what each student could achieve, and give the students a comprehensive tool kit for learning, to enable the students to become lifelong learners with a seamless ability to develop and grow.

Sandy realised that the school's aims applied to *all* young people, those whose backgrounds were damaged by emotional and financial poverty as well as those whose lives were financially and emotionally secure but where expectations, both within and outside school, often place an artificial ceiling on achievement – where success is graded by doing what you are asked, and not considering what it is that you might be able to do.

There were to be no quick fixes, though there was going to be success built into the very fabric of the school, allowing children to learn within the context of the political realities that are determined for schools wherever they are. There is a growing global agenda in education of national testing, league tables, perform-ance management and greater central control. Any innovation has to fulfil its own agenda as well as the criteria determined by the national programme of improvement. The success of the programme would surpass that agenda and engage the students' intrinsic desire to learn, which is as potent a force as sex, physical well-being or love, and yet all too often is not only a battle in school, but one that is tragically engaged and then lost.

Successful learning is the combination of feeling, thinking and doing. What we feel determines not only what we think, but how we think. The consequence of this powerful and irrepressible partnership is behaviour that may sometimes be intelligent or sometimes not. The control centre of learning is our emotions. They are the enablers and paradoxically the constrainers of what and how we learn. You can never *not* learn, though you can very powerfully constrain yourself from learning positive, constructive and generative lessons. We can only apply our tool kit for learning when we understand our emotions and how they dom-inate our development.

Breaking the blocks to learning would involve the students learning to use their emotional intelligence, and being empowered to succeed. The school set out to enable every child to become 'emotionally literate', to be able to describe their feelings and understand them, both for themselves and for others. All children would become leaders of their own emotional learning, able to use their power to build relationships and create opportunities for magical learning and per-sonal growth. Through this process of emotional development the students would begin to understand how they learn and be able to use tools that would make them a success both in the classroom and in their lives.

The school's programme was called the 'Passages Programme'. It was designed to confront the emotions that at different times we all bring to school and that block our learning and inhibit achievement. The emotions may be a deep-seated response to emotional memory, a consequence of events at home, the challenges of adolescence or the more mundane though no less influential impact of the daily environment – those feelings we have on rainy days when students come into our classroom having decided to find as many puddles as they can, basking in the adolescent bravado of being soaked to the skin. Our task, at this time, is to teach the curriculum, just as it is on the hot Friday afternoon when motivation is at an all-time low or when the children have just fought their way down a packed corridor from a slightly anarchistic time with the supply teacher.

All are occasions when the emotional state of the students is getting in the way of their learning. The students are feeling rebellious, lethargic, frustrated or just down about themselves. As a teacher you may even bring your own emotions, which may not be helping others to learn as well as you would want. The school's goal was to help the students become aware of how they feel and give them the tools to change it – to change the way they feel so that it will support their learning and not hinder it. Their goal was to develop the students' emotional literacy and emotional learning through the Passages Programme and within the subject-based curriculum.

During my discussions with Sandy we were interrupted twice as the intruder alarms went off and the two guards, armed and somewhat threatening, searched the corridors. This was clearly no ordinary school. Sandy told me of the gun battles that were a regular feature of her students' lives and the difficulties the staff found in helping students learn after they had been shot at! The school was University Heights High School in the Bronx, New York, and it has become a beacon school in emotional learning. The school has very particular problems. They work in a violent and intimidating atmosphere, though their approach has provided an insight into emotional learning that will benefit every child in every school. The emotional state of the students at University Heights may be exceptional and it may be prompted by extremes. The issue it highlights is the power of our emotions to enhance or inhibit our learning and the work that can successfully be done to empower students to take control of how they feel and use that knowledge to achieve success in the classroom and in life.

Emotional Intelligence is the ability to control and use our emotions to enhance our success in all aspects of our lives – success that is determined by a concept of intelligence that is broadly based, accessible to every student and capable of continual growth. Rather than another fad, another attempt to bring some light to the world of learning within schools, emotional intelligence draws on the strength of much that is good that has preceded it. EQ defines the nature of learning as being capable of creating a future where schools

> "Failing is not falling flat on your face, it's not getting up"
>
> Steve Cowley
> Vice President IBM Software

will fulfil and exceed the expectations placed upon them and the magic of learning will be available for every student and every teacher.

Emotional intelligence draws on the affective education movement, which has such a rich history but has been poorly understood and badly applied. It draws on the work of Howard Gardner in the field of multiple intelligences, Bandler and Grinder and the work that is ongoing in Neuro Linguistic Programming, and the accelerated learning movement so well described and chronicled by Alistair Smith and which has contributed so much to the recent development of learning. I shall describe in greater detail the contribution that these schools of thought have made to the development of EQ and how emotional intelligence has a history, a potency in the present and a great future in the development of learning in our schools and in the development of learning schools themselves.

The concept of emotions affecting how we learn is hardly new. It follows that being a leader of our emotions rather than a martyr to them will have a dramatic effect on our ability to succeed in the classroom and in our lives. However, where before the power of emotions in learning reflected in the affective learning movement was a matter of belief, it is now verifiable through empirical research into brain function.

I will briefly cover the major issues of how the brain responds to what we see, hear and feel to create emotion. Much of the understanding of emotional intelligence comes from a common-sense approach to our lives and learning. Some people, as they read this book, will feel that they have been using EQ in their professional and personal lives for years. Recent developments in brain research mean that you can understand why your work is having such an impact and develop your current practice. Those who have been struggling rather uneasily with a world dominated by IQ and a belief in 'filling empty vessels' can now find an alternative that will bring the magic back to children's learning, a new culture to classrooms and a sense of direction and purpose that will take much of the stress from teaching. Emotional intelligence has its roots in common sense and this is not to belittle it, but to give it enormous status and authority. It makes emotional intelligence accessible to everyone and with it the ability to develop our capacity to learn and succeed. Emotional intelligence may be common sense, but what it is not is common practice.

Learning is both natural and magical. We learn in order to achieve and succeed, in order to feel good about ourselves and our world. Learning is the single most potent feature of human motivation, growth and fulfilment. Understanding how people learn so fabulously well, how EQ is such a potent force, and how to translate that knowledge into classroom practice is the purpose of this book.

The book will engage three major questions and provide practical strategies to answer them (see Figure 0.1).

Addressing these areas is not a simple matter of providing worksheets on emotional intelligence and teaching it to children. The very essence of emotional intelligence is that it cannot be taught. It can, however, be learnt. The distinction means that some teachers will have to reflect on how they create learning in their

> "The only kind of learning that significantly influences behaviour is self discovered learning – truth that has been assimilated in experience"
>
> Carl Rogers
> Psychoanalyst

Figure 0.1: Three major questions

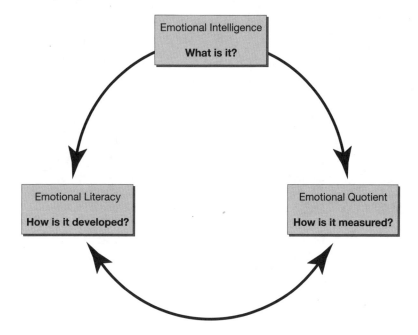

classrooms. Unleashing the power of learning is brought about by enabling, not enforcing. The teacher is the mediator of a process and not the force-feeder of information. This change of role is sometimes associated with a loss of control and therefore influence. The paradox is that by focusing on the process of learning and the teacher's role as mediator, the influence over learning increases and achievement rises.

The changes in reframing the relationship between teacher, student and the process of learning are straightforward, though profound. A colleague with whom I worked (whom I shall call Mary – not her real name) was wonderfully committed and dedicated. She helped every child in her charge to achieve great results. For her the journey of learning was less important than the destination. The consequence was that the students were less well prepared to decide where they should go next and less skilled at making the next journey themselves. Learning was a matter of compliance rather than commitment.

What Mary did not recognise was the impact that the journeys we take have on the destinations we arrive at. The interventions she made with the students ensured that the outcome of any project would be excellent. By doing this she was taking responsibility for the learning of the students. She was leaving her footprints on the very personal process of the students' growth and learning. The students were learning very little about how they learn and even less about how to apply that knowledge at different times and in different places.

After an emotional intelligence workshop on leadership in learning, Mary helped coach a programme for twelve- and thirteen-year-old students. One exercise involved a group problem-solving activity where the focus was on the process of learning. The relationship between the journey and the destination is that process (the journey) is merely product (the destination) in the making. Focus on the process and you will have as many high-quality products as you want. This will only happen if the children are allowed to take responsibility for their own learning.

Towards the end of this exercise, whilst I was observing the group, a student asked the teacher if they were allowed to fetch materials from outside to help solve the problem. Previously Mary would have either said yes or no, and if the answer had been 'yes' then she would have gone and done it for them. This time, she gestured with an open palm, engaged the child with a warmth I had never seen in her before and said "if you want to". With this simple phrase, the full opportunity and responsibility was placed squarely where it should be, with the student. The footprints were no longer there.

Emotional intelligence provides the opportunity for teachers and students to use the tools we all have to learn. It removes the inhibitions, self-doubt and negative behaviour that so restricts achievement for our students and traps teachers in a world of trying to shoe-horn learning, when all they need to do is open the door.

Emotional intelligence is the ability to rediscover what we previously had and then use it today. I have seen few three-year-olds who lack ambition, optimism, self-awareness or a fascination with learning. The reason they are so captivating, challenging and tiring is that they have all those qualities in such great abundance. The training and materials associated with this book will show you how you can help others rediscover the joy and magic of learning and how you can create those opportunities in every classroom. At a workshop on emotional intelligence, a colleague remarked that "the children came with a sense of wonder and left with a sense of wonderment". Emotional intelligence becomes the 'wow' of learning.

The programme for developing emotional learning is called 'The Magic Learning Programme'. The title may seem somewhat pretentious, though it has its roots in a very practical world. The title was given to me by a community worker in Greenwich who was achieving some remarkable results in getting truants to go back to school. I went down to meet her and find out what she was doing that was making her so successful. I spent the day with her and shared some of my own thoughts about learning and schools. As she was dropping me off at the tube station she asked again, with the sound of Bow Bells in her voice, "Now darlin', tell me again about this magic learning you've been doin'". She was so real, so committed and successful in what she was doing that she gave the phrase real power and potency – it stuck.

Magic Learning is a programme to give every student an emotional tool kit for success, to decide which emotions are going to allow the student to achieve their full potential and teach them to access those emotions when they need them. I can think of few things more frustrating than to feel confident and focused the day after the exam! We do not have to be slaves to our emotions, though all too often we allow ourselves to be just that. We accept how we feel as given when in reality we can feel just how we need to at any point in time. We can teach children to be emotional wizards, to feel what they need to feel to achieve success both in the classroom and in their lives.

The Magic Learning Programme (a series of programmes to develop learning styles and strategies for teachers, pupils and parents, not detailed in this book but available separately) is based on the premise that the five emotions of success are:

> Self-awareness
> Ambition
> Optimism
> Empathy
> Integrity

These have been derived from researching the five models of Emotional Intelligence detailed in Chapter Four. The list is not intended to gain universal approval. If students are given the opportunity to come up with their own list of success emotions and then use the tools in the Magic Learning Programme to deliver what they believe will bring success, then I will have achieved my goal.

Chapter One

Emotional Intelligence and the Structure of Learning

"In times of change the learners will inherit the earth, while the knowers will find themselves
beautifully equipped to deal with a world that no longer exists"
Eric Hoffer
Psychologist

Developing Emotional Intelligence will remove the barriers to learning that we all build as we grow. We build barriers to protect ourselves from a changing sense of failure, from a view of ourselves increasingly dependent on the approbation of our peers. We move as we grow from being a question mark in our approach to learning to being a full stop. This metaphor was first coined by Edward de Bono in his book *Teach Your Child How to Think*, and is a valuable insight into our changing self as learner. Because we have been someone different in relation to learning means that we can always go back there if we choose. In order to give people that choice, it is important to beak down Emotional Intelligence into the dual parts of emotional literacy and emotional learning. Emotional literacy allows you to describe and understand your emotions and those of others. Emotional learning is the application of the power of emotion, controlling this potent force and using it for the benefit of all aspects of our lives.

Becoming a fabulous learner requires a deep understanding of both emotional intelligence and the process of learning. There is a growing and not very helpful tendency in education to break learning down into its component parts in the misguided belief you can then put it back together again and re-create the whole. It is rather like trying to put the pieces of a broken mirror back together and expecting to have a perfect image. Emotional Intelligence can only be fully understood as an integrated part of the process of learning and is not something that can be bolted on like another literacy or numeracy hour.

Bringing together Emotional Intelligence and learning creates something that is different from the perceptions that may abound when they are considered separately. Beer and lemonade make shandy, yellow and red orange, a girl and a boy a couple. By adding one thing to another something new is created. Emotional intelligence and the process of learning will look, feel and sound different when they are together. The perception of learning and the achievement of personal excellence in our schools will then perhaps begin to make sense.

Learning is a process that has both breadth and depth, though all too often learning in school is reduced to its end product, the learning outcome. The magic and

Figure 1.1: What is learning?

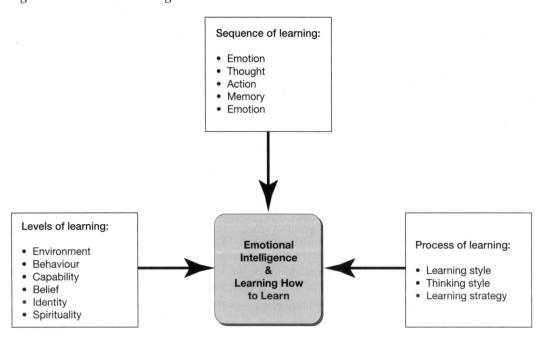

power of learning are in the process and the successful outcomes are then a natural consequence of that focus. Looking at outcomes does not help us to understand the process. Looking at the outcomes of learning actively blocks our ability to see what we need to see about the process of learning. We focus on destination at the expense of the journey and the consequence is that we paradoxically often do not end up where we want to be and certainly not where we need to be.

Seeing learning as outcomes camouflages and distracts our attention from the process of learning and sends many students away from school surrounded by negative beliefs about themselves. It is not the destination any school wants, but it is where many end up. It is not what schools are doing that is the issue but how they are doing it. Students are not able to consider their relationship with learning because it is clouded by what they are being driven to achieve. A poem I read, about a woman considering leaving her partner, serves as a good metaphor for the relationship students often perceive they have with learning. It read:

> Shall I leave him?
> I'll write a letter
> Or should I,
> Get to know him better?

Too many students are getting the letter before they have got to know learning better.

Students turn off from school and underachieve in a restless, indifferent and sometimes aggressive way because the drive towards outcomes comes between the students and their powerful and natural force to learn. Get the process of learning right and you will be showered by all the outcomes you want. Focus on the outcomes and the students will remain like some people walking home after a long night at the pub – definitely somewhere, though never quite able to remember how or why they got there.

The temptation to look at outcomes as the main evidence of successful learning is powerful, though tragically it is dis-empowering thousands of young people and leaving them never understanding how they can release the fabulous potential they have to learn. Schools may be looking for success in an area where the light shines brightly but it may not be the place that the key to success in the classroom and in life can actually be found.

There is a modern version of an old Sufi story where a passer-by sees a drunk on all fours looking for something under a street light. The passer-by watched for a moment or two and then asked the drunk what he was looking for. He said he had lost his door key and the stranger spent several minutes looking in vain for the key. Feeling that the key might not be found, he asked the drunk where he had lost it. "By my door", he replied. "Then why don't you look over there?", replied the stranger. "Because there is no light by my door", replied the drunk.

The next part of this chapter on the structure of learning will look at the different parts of learning and how each can be made to work in a way that will bring them together with a sense of congruence, to create a dynamic process in a school environment.

The Sequence of Learning

Why are we better at some subjects than others? I wasn't born with the belief that I am better at history than I am at maths and that someone has been trying to teach me the chemistry syllabus backwards. I learned it. Not by myself but with the help of others whom I let persuade me of these things. The potential we have in school to create learning is enormous. The power we exercise to stop learning is frightening.

> "No one can make you feel inferior without your consent"
>
> Eleanor Roosevelt
> Diplomat and Humanitarian

The sequence of learning can be made positive and constructive through interventions in the process. I will describe the sequence and give some examples of the sort of interventions that will make a difference. At this stage the interventions focus more on the cognitive aspects of learning, though it is impossible to look just at cognition without looking at emotion. There is no thinking without feeling and no feeling without thinking. The balance is addressed in later chapters where I will focus more on emotion and then bring them fully together in Chapter Six, on the Magic Learning Programme (the programme itself is available separately). Despite having extolled the virtues of a holistic approach to learning, I shall now ignore my own good advice and describe the separate parts, which will bring with it some degree of temporary artificiality.

Figure 1.2 Sequence of Learning

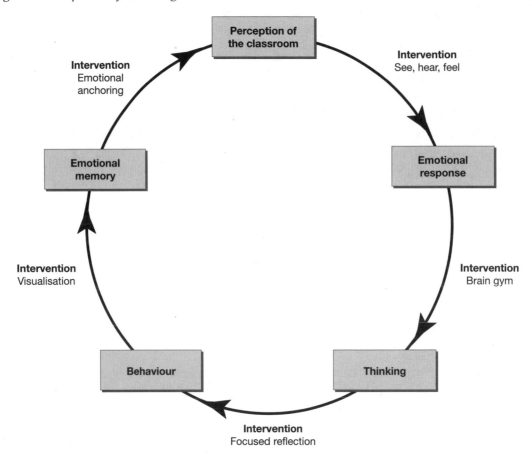

It is worth spending some time on the stages in the sequence of learning, partly because of the old adage about 'starts' and 'the wrong foot' and partly because it is in the individual stages that learning will be developed and teachers will begin to exert the influence that their status demands.

Perceptions of the Classroom

How students develop their perceptions of the classroom, deciding whether it is an environment where they can learn, or whether it is a hostile place intended for others, is described in a model of learning developed by Robert Dilts and outlined in his book *Dynamic Learning*. It is called the ROLE model. This stands for:

- **R**epresentational systems – How we use our senses
- **O**rientation – Whether we are looking out into the world or inside ourselves
- **L**inks – Between our senses
- **E**ffect – Of our learning

1. *Representational systems*

These are the systems through which we 'represent' the world to ourselves, through which we develop our personal perceptions of the world. We experience the world and learn through our senses. The primary senses are Visual (sight), Auditory (sound) and Kinaesthetic (feeling), though there are also gustatory (taste) and olfactory (smell). We all use a combination of these systems to take in information about the world and create

> "To learn anything fast and effectively you need to see it, hear it and feel it"
>
> Tony Stockwell
> Educational Psychologist

our perceptions of it. In the same way, students will take in information about the classroom and form their perceptions of it. We use the full range of representational systems available to us, though we will have a preference. I may be a visual learner, an auditory learner or a kinaesthetic learner.

2. *Orientation*

In order to learn we focus our senses either externally or internally – either toward the outside world or internally, by remembering past experiences and by constructing new ones. Our learning is contextualised either in past experience or in imagined futures. The importance of this is that the representational (Visual/Auditory/Kinaesthetic) systems and our orientation (internal/external) come together and then are notorious for getting in the way of the learning relationship between the teacher and the student.

Each individual will have preferred representational systems and, if they are unaware of this, will express themselves in terms of their preference, often to the bemusement of someone who is thinking in a different way. Consider, for example, the following exchange between a student and a teacher about a homework project. The teacher usually uses their *visual* skills to understand the world, and this is reflected in their language ('see', 'looked', 'clearer picture'). The student has a preference for *kinaesthetic* learning and uses vocabulary that reflects *feelings*, emotional and physical:

Teacher: *"I **see** you haven't completed your homework."*

Student: *"I had a lot to do this week and I **felt** I ought to prioritise my Geography which needs to be in by Wednesday."*

Teacher: *"If you **looked** more closely you would **see** that there were ways you could have got both done."*

Student: *"I **feel** that you don't really appreciate the **pressure** I am under and that you are being rather **harsh**."*

Teacher: *"I think you need to **see** the way ahead more **clearly** and have a better **picture** of where you are going and what you want."*

The difference between visual and kinaesthetic language may seem slight and inconsequential but it has a remarkable effect, making communication difficult and often creating misunderstanding. By listening to the sort of language people use and trying to use similar vocabulary, be it visual, auditory or kinaesthetic, we greatly increase the power of our communication, we lay the foundation of positive relationships and greatly increase the effectiveness of our teaching. *The only message is the one that is received,* and this is all too often very different from the one that we intend. If the outcome of the exchange between the student and the teacher is that the student goes away feeling resentful and devalued because they were not understood, then this will have a profound impact on their perceptions of the subject, school and their ability to learn. The relationship between the student and teacher is crucial to the success of learning.

3. Links

We learn best by taking in experiences through more than one of our senses. We construct our experiences and our learning by either linking our representational systems or layering them one on top of another. The layering is sometimes called synaesthesia. Linking might be when you hear a piece of music that prompts an emotional response because it reminds you of a strong experience in your past, such as the music when you first fell in love or the theme tune of your favourite television programme. Both will be associated with a kinaesthetic response. I recently saw an article in a magazine about 'smelling your way to success'. The company would sell you a variety of aromas that you could smell when you felt good and had achieved something positive. Smelling the aromas in the future will help to bring back the emotional state you had when you had been successful, increasing your chances of repeating the feat. We use these skills of using a stimulus to evoke an emotional response all the time in our lives, though all too often to reinforce negative beliefs. The same process that comes so naturally can be used to build on success and become a powerful tool in emotional learning.

It may be that you layer one representational system on another. Choosing the colours to redecorate your house, you may feel that "the brown is too heavy", linking visual and kinaesthetic, or listening to music you feel "that was a really smooth piece", linking kinaesthetic and auditory. It was said that Mozart would hear, see and feel his music. The process Mozart used to learn was powerful and he clearly understood how to learn. There is a book by Michael Gelb called *How to think like Leonardo da Vinci.* It is a good read, and he argues that da Vinci was able to achieve what he did as a great painter, scientist, inventor, astronomer, poet, because he understood the process of learning. He could do what he did because he understood how to learn. Understand the process and the outcomes you want will follow.

4. Effect

The effect of learning is not only that you have learnt a particular piece of knowledge but that you have understood how you have done it and can apply that skill in the future.

The first building block of learning is the sequence of learning. To ensure that the sequence has positive outcomes the teacher can intervene between each part of that sequence in order to increase the chances of success.

This is not intended to be a comprehensive list of interventions; they are simply examples of what is possible. More detailed strategies are in the Magic Learning Programme available separately.

Emotional Response

How do we get emotions? All too often our emotional state is treated as a given. We feel what we feel and we had better get on with it. The consequence of this wholly erroneous attitude is that little is done to help students create a positive emotional response. They are left to deal, often inadequately, with avoidable problems.

This is highlighted in the way schools often conduct exams. There are regulations that must be fulfilled, though much of the organisation of examinations is conducted in a way that guarantees stress, anxiety, fear and inevitable under-achievement. When schools have invested so much time and effort in preparing students for their exams, why do they then rock the boat so violently? The gathering of students together, the silence demanded on entrance (why not play music? – the effect of music on emotional state is well documented), the banning of mascots that the students powerfully associate with comfort and reassurance, the harsh command-focused tones at the start (why not spend a moment getting the students to visualise success? – see later in the chapter for this valuable technique) – so much more could be done to create a positive emotional response to the demands of examinations and thereby raise levels of achievement.

The same applies to the way students associate their perceptions of many classrooms with stress, anxiety and impending failure. The school bell is a metaphor for much that inhibits learning in school. If teachers really cannot be trusted to tell the time, why do schools have to have a noise that is so abrupt and jarring to denote the change of lessons? Have you ever paused by a ringing school bell and felt relaxed and positive about the warm embrace of its sound? Why are children expected to finish all lessons at the same time and fight their way down overcrowded corridors? I once wrote a school timetable based on departments choosing their lesson length based on units of 25 minutes. Not only did it acknowledge the differing time demands of learning Technology and Modern Languages, it also spread the movement of students so that they could walk and not fight their way to their classrooms. It had the wonderful consequence of making the school bell inoperable except at the start and end of the day.

We all associate what we see, hear and feel around us with an emotional response. An event comes wrapped like a sweet with emotion around it. It may be the response to exams, the school bell, a piece of music that makes us remember a specific event, the sight of a smile or the first Christmas decorations of the year. These are called anchors, where an event has an emotion anchored to it. Classrooms and the way we teach in them generate emotional responses, which aren't always positive. It is possible to do far more and make a powerful impact on students' success in learning.

Thinking

The next stage in the learning cycle is the way we think. We develop our sense of the world, create an emotional response to what we see, hear and feel and then think about it.

The way we think varies from one person to another. There are various taxonomies of thinking. I have used Gregorc's thinking styles as a tool to consider the thinking styles of staff and students. It is described in the Magic Learning Programme and then adapted to make it usable for students and staff. It is important to raise our self-awareness so that we understand how we individually pass through the sequence of learning: to know what we do and to know that others do it differently; to know that we can understand from others about how they think and learn and try different strategies.

Learning Behaviour

A lot of time and energy are spent in trying to modify students' behaviour that is seen as getting in the way of their learning and the learning of others. The intervention is usually aimed at the behaviour, rather than the learning, and as a result usually doesn't work. Poor behaviour is often to do with a lack of understanding of the learning process. Help students to understand how they learn and how they can mediate in their own learning and they have a powerful tool for life. I have run learning programmes with disaffected 15- and 16-year-olds where I have been successful in turning them into empowered learners, which has then brought about remarkable changes in behaviour.

Emotional Memory

We remember events, places, skills and people, though most dramatically we remember how we felt at different times or in response to events in our lives. That emotional memory determines how we will probably respond in the future. If something doesn't go well, we will remember the feelings we associate with failure and do all we can to avoid having them again.

We all have things we have learnt to believe we are not very good at. We cannot sing, or draw, are not very good at maths or at school in general. To ignore these

> "I have not failed 10,000 times. I have successfully found 10,000 ways that don't work"
>
> Thomas Edison
> Inventor and Physicist

8

memories and carry on teaching a subject or a skill is to waste precious time. The efforts will be rejected. However, because emotional memories are a matter of choice we can revisit them and change the association with a particular event. Seeing failure as feedback and a reflection of 'work in progress' allows learning to continue. This is a skill that can be built into the activity of every classroom where students are aware of their emotions and can use them to help their learning rather than have them hinder it.

My three-year-old daughter Abigail is a fabulous learner. She can swim, ride a bike, read, write and do complex maths. She just can't do them *yet*. Her attitude to her learning is to see feedback and not failure and therefore her learning cycle continues. Schools must learn how to provide feedback rather than teaching failure. The Magic Learning Programme will empower students to see their learning in a different way and to continue their learning so that they do become the very best that they can possibly be and understand that this goal is a lifetime's mission.

Seeing learning as a cycle where interventions can be made at different stages is crucial if students are to fulfil the vast untapped potential that they have. It is also essential to see learning as something that can always be revisited and changed. To paraphrase George Eliot, "it is never too late to become who we want to be". Understanding learning and the powerful role of emotion in that process is essential if we are to empower students to become lifelong learners.

Interventions to see Great Learning in your Classroom

The purpose is to outline some of the ways in which different learning styles can be reflected in the interventions that can take place in the classroom. The detail and substance of those interventions are contained in the Magic Learning Programme.

1. Students' perception – emotional response
a. Auditory
We all know from personal experience how we use music in our lives to reflect the way we feel. We also know how others use music deliberately to change the way we feel. Film-makers have known of the power of music and have used it to dramatic effect for years. The value and importance of the sound track's role in making you engage emotionally with the drama are reflected in the Oscars that are given over to this item alone. Theme tunes to soap operas start to get the audience in the mood for the expectation of what is to come. The depth of engagement with the music could be judged if someone suggested changing the theme tune to *Coronation Street* or *EastEnders*. There might be something of an outcry. The fabulous 1950s music introducing *Sports Report* on the radio was changed some years ago. There was such a large protest that it had to be reinstated.

Sports men and women use music to help to motivate themselves and often the crowd. Few Rugby League teams emerge on to the pitch to the strains of a Bach violin concerto. There may, however, be some learning about the diminishing power of repetition in some circumstances. I think that if I hear 'The Hero Inside Myself' at one more sports ground or training venue I may do serious damage to the local PA system. Despite all we know and experience about the power of music and the theory behind the Mozart effect in learning, music is rarely used as an intervention strategy in learning. When it is used it usually reflects only a small portion of its potential as a tool for learning.

People have specific behaviour patterns associated with music and yet the nearest we get to it in school is the noise of the bell. Most learning takes place at the beginning and end of a learning period. Play music that children will associate with starting or ending learning sessions within a lesson. The students will begin to learn before you want them to. Over 90% of learning is subconscious; music is a powerful tool in gaining access to that subconscious ability to learn. Decide on the emotional response that the group needs, to calm down and concentrate, to be invigorated, to be more externally or internally focused, and play them the music that will work. Even if 60% of the class respond, they will start to create the culture that will take the other 40% with them. Music is a powerful and grossly underused intervention in learning.

b. Visual

Visual learning and visual memory allow a real impact to be made on the students' perception of their learning environment. Material displayed in the classroom will be taken in by the students at an unconscious level. This will be helped if the material is placed just above eye level and changed regularly to stop it becoming invisible to even the unconscious eye.

A colleague taped off a small part of the board in her room with masking tape. At the start of the lesson she writes the aims and objectives for the lesson in that square. It is a quite remarkable centre of attention whilst it is being filled in, and in review at the end when the aims are removed if they have been achieved. Simple, easy and it has a great impact.

Visualising is a tremendous skill that we have that can be used in all sorts of ways to enhance our learning. It can be used to develop specific skills, for example spelling. I describe this later in the book, though it is worth saying at this stage that most good spellers are visual learners. They see spelling mistakes shining out from a page. Knowing this, it is very easy to teach non-visual learners the skills and strategies they need to be great spellers.

Displaying the content of the lesson as a mind map has the effect of making it visually powerful and gives the students a chance to model their use. The rules for mind maps are well documented and they reflect the rules for visual learning when it is effective. The use of colour, size, symbols rather than words, movement and exaggeration, all help visual learning to be successful.

c. Kinaesthetic

Learning in school is often free of kinaesthetic experiences because of the lack of space or the erroneous view that a particular subject does not lend itself to kinaesthetic learning. There is increasing evidence that many underachieving boys are kinaesthetic learners. You can learn to spell using kinaesthetic techniques, tracing words with a finger or have someone trace the words on you. Brain Gym is a great kinaesthetic experience accessible in every classroom. Changing physiology changes the perception of learning. Standing up to do oral group work will change what happens. Experiment, have the students do something different. This very act of doing something different will help them to 'grow their brain'.

Visualising experience is a very good substitute for not actually doing something. It can give a student a sense of an experience and allow them to understand how they would feel if.... Kinaesthetic experience is possible in every classroom and will make learning accessible for all students.

2.   *Emotional response – thinking*

There is still the National Curriculum to teach, and having a class of meditative students hoping that their subconscious learning will see them through may not be seen as taking your professional duties as far as you should. Brain Gym is a great way of getting children thinking. The theory is that by engaging in a physical activity that uses both sides of your body and is an activity that you don't usually do, it is outside your comfort zone of learning (swinging both your arms may not do it), and you therefore engage both sides of the brain, each of which contributes different qualities to how and what we learn. We need both of them to learn and having them working together is a great help. The physical activity helps to lay down neural pathways that link both sides of the brain and enable us to think more effectively.

Brain Gym will have a dramatic affect on your class, both emotionally and cognitively. There are books of Brain Gym exercises on the market, but to give you a flavour and something to try, here are three.

a.   Alphabet

Write the letters of the alphabet on the board and randomly write an L or an R or a B under each letter. Ask the class to stand, give them a slow rhythm to start with and call out the letters. They raise their left arm if the letter has an L under it, their right arm if the letter has an R under it, or both for a B. Repeat it faster and then backwards. It will take 3 minutes and you will see, hear and feel the difference.

b.   Air names

Again ask the class to stand and write their names in the air using their preferred hand (i.e. the hand they usually write with). Now they should write it in the air using their other hand and then using both. Now, using both hands, they should write their names backwards.

c. Lazy 8s

Ask the class to describe an 8 in the air using their preferred hand. Now they should put the 8 on its side. Repeat the exercise with the other hand, with both hands and backwards.

You may wish to try Brain Gym. Just have fun – and tell the students why they are having fun too.

3. *Thinking – behaviour*

Visualising what you are going to do is a well-known technique in psychology; it is used extensively in sport, where it works to optimise performance. Optimal performance is the focus of classroom activity and will be made far more likely for far more students by using visualisation skills.

You are not asking the students to do something they haven't done thousands of times before. They may just not have realised it. Get them used to having their own video screen: ask them to look up and to the left to see it (learning physiology is important); ask them to run a video of what they have been asked to do, seeing the task through to completion. They should see what problems they encounter, then rerun the video, solving them. You may at first feel uncomfortable asking the children to access their screens; they won't, and will take to it as if they had been doing it all their lives, which of course they have. It is important to help the students bridge their skills so that they can apply them whenever they want, and don't just associate them with the classroom.

4. *Behaviour – emotional memory*

Your students will bring all sorts of emotional memories of school and learning to your classroom. Build up the wrong ones over a period of time and you have the next generation of parents who are physically and emotionally unable to come into school to support their children's learning.

At the end of the lesson, put on some gentle reflective music, playing softly; ask the students to relax and remember the lesson. For younger students you may help them with the behaviour of relaxation by asking them to close their eyes and put their head on their arms.

Take the students through the lesson, reminding them of what they have seen, heard and felt during the lesson. This is important in order to include all the students, who will have a variety of preferred representational systems. Remind them of what they have learnt, the content and what they may have learnt about how they learn.

The effect will be to deepen their learning, helping to access their long-term memory and create a sense of relaxed focus in the students, for which the next teacher who has them will love you.

5. *Emotional memory – perception of the classroom*

When you start your lesson, remind the students not only of the content of what they have previously done, but the learning about learning and how they felt. Bring back the positive emotional memories that they are then able to build on. Should your previous lesson not have gone quite to plan, decide on the personal, emotional resources you want the students to have today. These may be confidence, risk taking, optimism, determination, fun and so on. Decide on your focus and ask them to remind themselves of occasions when they have been determined, for example. The very act of revisiting that memory will help to reunite the students with their own ability and contribute to their learning in the lesson. There are ways of deepening this process that are covered in the Magic Learning Programme.

Interventions in the process of learning are powerful tools in developing individual excellence. They are also great fun and empower you with tremendous influence over learning, by lowering your voice and your stress levels too.

The whole process of learning is the same in the classroom as it is in any aspect of life. The tools you give the children in learning to learn and developing their own emotional intelligence will be as valuable for them when they are confronting those life-changing issues of adolescence as in the life opportunities created by success in school.

I have recently had the pleasure of taking my children to the local skateboarding park, my son to skateboard and my daughters to roller-blade. On the first visit both my son and eldest daughter were able to come down the smallest slope by themselves. Both had had to confront some anxiety, despite Joe being clad like a Roman gladiator. The second time we went they had both 'forgotten' about their success and were remembering the anxiety that they had previously felt. Neither would come down without a hand being held and Joe was reluctant to get on the slope at all. We practised visualising them being successful on their previous visit, though anxiety and fear of falling was still stopping their learning. I noticed my daughter squeezing her thumb and asked her what she was doing. She said she was remembering what it was like to hold my hand, which gave her confidence. This act of remembering by establishing a kinaesthetic anchor is a very powerful way of controlling our emotional memories to support learning rather than allowing our memories to inhibit it. Hannah felt calmer and began to make some progress.

Joe and Hannah have the usual healthy amount of sibling rivalry, though Joe was able to listen to how his sister had done something and was prepared to try it. Focusing on process allowed real collaborative learning to take place, as it is far less threatening than sharing outcomes. You share process and you can be different as there are always thousands of ways of doing the same thing. Focus on outcomes and you are straight into better and worse.

> "Whether you believe you can or you can't you are probably right"
>
> Henry Ford
> Automobile engineer
> and manufacturer

Joe started remembering the confidence he had when he held my hand and started skating down the slope. My other daughter, Abigail, is three and so has not learnt to let emotions inhibit her aspiration or anything dampen her optimism. She skated down the slope having wonderful fun in her learning. The danger is that to some degree she will learn to inhibit her learning through memory of negative experience. The wonderful thing is that by developing a sense of her own emotional intelligence she will also learn to recognise what she can change in order to maintain her capacity as a fabulous learner.

Having got home, Hannah had to feed the guinea pigs in the garage. The door was stuck and as she came back indoors she said, with a somewhat sardonic look on her face, "you know that self-belief stuff … it won't work on the garage door". Ah well, work in progress!

The Process of Learning

Learning Styles

The second of the major building blocks of learning is the learning style we have. Learning style should not be confused with thinking style and learning strategy.

Learning style describes:

- The way you make sense of the learning environment – whether you have a preference to learn by looking (Visual), listening (Auditory) or doing (Kinaesthetic). You will not have one learning style to the total exclusion of others, but you will have a preference.
- Your learning style is probably inherited, though it is certainly possible and desirable to develop your skills in each of the main areas.

Thinking styles are:

- The way you think within your style of learning.
- The most valuable classification is probably Gregorc's, which is described in more detail later.

Learning strategies are:

- What you do in order to make the most of your learning style. You can continually change and develop your learning strategies.
- Learning strategies will develop your thinking capacity within a range of thinking styles.

Identifying Learning Styles

Identifying how students learn is crucial if the interventions that a teacher makes are to be successful. Realising that most students will have a preference enables you to group students so that they learn more strategies about their preferred style. Also, they can begin to develop skills in other styles of learning that they would not normally choose to use.

The following questionnaire will help to give baseline information and raise awareness for students about their learning. There is also an activity that may help you correlate learning style against achievement. There is some evidence that many underachieving boys are kinaesthetic learners. It is not that they can't learn, or are any less motivated than any other group. It is just that they are not learning how to use a variety of learning styles. The way learning is being organised in many classrooms is predominantly auditory or visual. It is as though their television is not properly tuned.

Learning style questionnaire
This is an opportunity to explore a little more how you learn. Answer the following questions. Put down your first answer and try not to pause too long on each one. There is no right or wrong answer.

1. *When you get in touch with someone, do you prefer to:*

   a) *Meet them face to face* . . . .❑
   b) *Talk on the telephone* . . . .❑
   c) *Get together and do something* . . . .❑

2. *What do you notice most about people?*

   a) *How they stand and move* . . . .❑
   b) *How they look or dress* . . . .❑
   c) *How they sound when they talk* . . . .❑

3. *How do you learn most easily?*

   a) *By listening to what people say* . . . .❑
   b) *By watching someone show you what to do* . . . .❑
   c) *By doing something* . . . .❑

4. *When you are angry, do you:*

    a) *Say very little but hold your anger inside* . . . . ☐
    b) *Shout and argue very loudly* . . . . ☐
    c) *Clench your fists and grit your teeth* . . . . ☐

5. *When you are talking to someone, do you:*

    a) *Use your hands a lot and make gestures* . . . . ☐
    b) *Enjoy listening but get impatient to talk* . . . . ☐
    c) *Stop talking and listening and do something* . . . . ☐

6. *When you have a lot to do, do you:*

    a) *Make lists either on paper or in your mind* . . . . ☐
    b) *Keep telling yourself that you have things to do* . . . . ☐
    c) *Do what needs to be done* . . . . ☐

7. *When you read, do you prefer:*

    a) *Action stories* . . . . ☐
    b) *Descriptive stories and imagine the scenes* . . . . ☐
    c) *Reading conversations between people* . . . . ☐

8. *When you are remembering someone, do you:*

    a) *Remember names* . . . . ☐
    b) *Remember faces* . . . . ☐
    c) *Remember how you felt about them* . . . . ☐

9. *When you have some free time, do you:*

    a) *Watch the TV, video or go to the movies* . . . . ☐
    b) *Do something active* . . . . ☐
    c) *Listen to music or read* . . . . ☐

10. *What would make you suspect that someone is lying to you:*

    a) *The way they look* . . . . ☐
    b) *The sound of their voice* . . . . ☐
    c) *A feeling you get* . . . . ☐

Learning style score sheet
1. *Look at the answers you have given to each of the questions.*
2. *Decide whether you have answered a), b), or c).*
3. *Give yourself 1 point for each answer.*
4. *Put a 1 in the box that is the same as your answer, in either a), b) or c).*
5. *Add up your totals at the end.*
6. *The column with the highest total will show you how you prefer to learn, either Visually (V), Auditorily (A) or Kinaesthetically (K).*

			V	A	K
1.	a)	b)	c)	☐	☐	☐
2.	b)	c)	a)	☐	☐	☐
3.	b)	a)	c)	☐	☐	☐
4.	a)	b)	c)	☐	☐	☐
5.	a)	b)	c)	☐	☐	☐
6.	a)	b)	c)	☐	☐	☐
7.	b)	c)	a)	☐	☐	☐
8.	b)	a)	c)	☐	☐	☐
9.	a)	c)	b)	☐	☐	☐
10.	a)	b)	c)	☐	☐	☐

Total   ___ ___ ___

Learning table
Get into groups of four. Your teacher will give each group a title, either a number, a letter, a colour or a day of the week. Share your learning style results within your group and record them. Find someone from another group classification and record their results. Do this until you have recorded the results of each of the group classifications. As you collect the data from other students in different groups, fill in this form underlining either a "b" for boy or "g" for girl, showing where you got the information from.

- What do your results suggest about how we learn?
- How can you use this information to help your own learning?

Learning table

My results	V	A	K
Results 1 B/G	☐	☐	☐
Results 2 B/G	☐	☐	☐
Results 3 B/G	☐	☐	☐
Results 4 B/G	☐	☐	☐
Results 5 B/G	☐	☐	☐
Results 6 B/G	☐	☐	☐
Results 7 B/G	☐	☐	☐
Results 8 B/G	☐	☐	☐
Results 9 B/G	☐	☐	☐
Results 10 B/G	☐	☐	☐
Results 11 B/G	☐	☐	☐
Results 12 B/G	☐	☐	☐
Results 13 B/G	☐	☐	☐
Results 14 B/G	☐	☐	☐
Results 15 B/G	☐	☐	☐
Results 16 B/G	☐	☐	☐
Total	—	—	—
Girls	—	—	—
Boys	—	—	—

Knowing someone's preferred learning style does not tell you how students are learning at a particular point in time. Preference does not mean the same as exclusivity. I may prefer one food to another though I enjoy a wide ranging diet. So it is with learning. I will have a preferred learning style though I will use other styles in different contexts and sometimes to verify my learning in my preferred mode. This again is going to be invaluable in helping to develop the students' understanding of how they learn and a powerful tool in developing learning relationships between the teacher and the student. It will help students to understand the physiology of learning and give a greater insight for staff into mediation in learning.

Two important pieces of evidence exist to help you determine how someone is learning: (1) their eye movements and (2) the language they use.

Do this simple test with a student or a friend and watch the movement of their eyes. Ask them the following questions:

1. What colour is your front door?
2. What colour would you like your next car to be?
3. What is the theme tune of your favourite TV show?
4. How did it feel when you first fell in love?
5. What job would you do if you had your choice over again and money was no object?

Add as many more questions as you like that ask your partner to consider seeing something, hearing something or feeling (either emotion or sensation) in the past and in the future.

The eye movements you will see are described below. Sometimes they may be a mirror image of this, particularly in left-handed people.

Looking up and to their right

They are constructing an image of something in the future

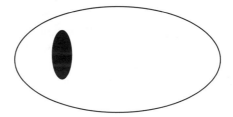

Looking up and to their left

They are constructing an image of something they are remembering

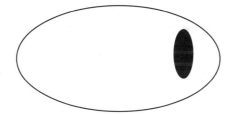

Looking down and to their right

They are remembering a kinaesthetic experience

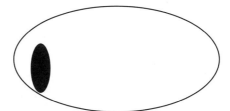

Looking down and to their left

They are discussing an issue with themselves and deciding what the options will feel like

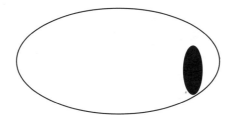

Looking side to side, neither up nor down

They are remembering or
creating an auditory experience

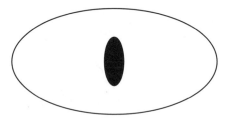

The value of this is enormous, firstly in developing learning strategies with students. If you can see that they are trying to learn something kinaesthetically and it isn't working, you can help them find other strategies. If you are counselling children, it is a powerful tool in helping them to understand what is happening to them, at perhaps a difficult time.

Thinking Styles

Our learning style, how we take in information, is then built on by how we use it. Our thinking style helps us to understand the skills we have to use the information we have taken in.

Below are some examples of exercises you can use with students to help them understand their thinking style and some of the strengths they have as learners. They form part of the Magic Learning Programme. Students are encouraged to keep a 'Learning Journal' to help them identify and analyse learning strategies.

How do I think?
Read each of the words and mark the two that best describe you.

1. a. Imaginative ....☐
   b. Investigative ....☐
   c. Realistic ....☐
   d. Analytical ....☐

2. a. Organised ....☐
   b. Adaptable ....☐
   c. Critical ....☐
   d. Inquisitive ....☐

3. a. Debating ....☐
   b. Getting to the point ....☐
   c. Creating ....☐
   d. Relating ....☐

4. a. Personal . . . . ❏
    b. Practical . . . . ❏
    c. Academic . . . . ❏
    d. Adventurous . . . . ❏

5. a. Precise . . . . ❏
    b. Flexible . . . . ❏
    c. Systematic . . . . ❏
    d. Inventive . . . . ❏

6. a. Sharing . . . . ❏
    b. Orderly . . . . ❏
    c. Sensible . . . . ❏
    d. Independent . . . . ❏

7. a. Competitive . . . . ❏
    b. Perfectionist . . . . ❏
    c. Co-operative . . . . ❏
    d. Logical . . . . ❏

8. a. Intellectual . . . . ❏
    b. Sensitive . . . . ❏
    c. Hard working . . . . ❏
    d. Risk taking . . . . ❏

9. a. Reader . . . . ❏
    b. People person . . . . ❏
    c. Problem solver . . . . ❏
    d. Planner . . . . ❏

10. a. Memorise . . . . ❏
    b. Associate . . . . ❏
    c. Think through . . . . ❏
    d. Originate . . . . ❏

11. a. Changer . . . . ❏
    b. Judger . . . . ❏
    c. Spontaneous . . . . ❏
    d. Wants direction . . . . ❏

12. a. Communicating . . . . ❏
    b. Discovering . . . . ❏
    c. Cautious . . . . ❏
    d. Reasoning . . . . ❏

13. a. Challenging . . . . ❏
    b. Practising . . . . ❏
    c. Caring . . . . ❏
    d. Examining . . . . ❏

14. a. Completing work ....❏
    b. Seeing possibilities ....❏
    c. Gaining ideas ....❏
    d. Interpreting ....❏

15. a. Doing ....❏
    b. Feeling ....❏
    c. Thinking ....❏
    d. Experimenting ....❏

Thinking styles score sheet
Circle the letter of the words you chose. Add the totals up in each of the columns. The box with the highest score describes the way you most often think.

1.	C	D	A	B
2.	A	C	B	D
3.	B	A	D	C
4.	B	C	A	D
5.	A	C	B	D
6.	B	C	A	D
7.	B	D	C	A
8.	C	A	B	D
9.	D	A	B	D
10.	A	C	B	D
11.	D	B	C	A
12.	C	D	A	B
13.	B	D	C	A
14.	A	C	D	B
15.	A	C	B	D
	Total ____	Total ____	Total ____	Total ____
	1.	**2.**	**3.**	**4.**

1. Organised Problem Solver
2. Logical Problem Solver
3. Team Building Problem Solver
4. Skilled Problem Solver

Source: *The Learning Revolution*

How do I Learn?

Developing my thinking

Time	*45 minutes*
Groups	*Working in changing pairs*
Resources	*Developing your thinking activity sheet*
Process	

1. *Review the results of the thinking styles sheet. Everyone will have something they can say they are good at.*
2. *Ask the class to show who is better at each of the thinking styles and ask them to get into pairs with someone who has a similar strength. Are there any gender issues in the thinking strengths of individuals?*
3. *Work through the 'Developing your Thinking' activity sheet. First, find someone who has the same major strength as you in their thinking and answer the questions in that area of thinking. Give as much detail as you can as someone else will be depending on your level of expertise.*
4. *Find someone who has the same strength in your second major area and work with them. If your first partner has the same second strength as you then you may decide to stay with them.*
5. *Now find someone who is good at the two areas where you are not so hot. Write down in your Learning Journal anything that they do that you think may be worth trying.*
6. *Decide on one area that you are not very good at, at the moment, and set yourself a task for homework.*
7. *Write up your task in your Learning Journal.*

Activity sheet: Developing your thinking
Organised problem solver

You are 'Hot' at:

- Organising
- Finding out details and information
- Making big things small so you can work through them a bit at a time
- Getting things ready so that you can work well

Your task, should you wish to accept it, is:

1. Think of an event, either in school, at home or with your friends, when you put your strengths to good use. This might be an event like helping to organise your birthday, or something that you were good at over a period of time, like organising your homework, looking after a pet, or getting ready for a club.

2. When you have both thought about something you organised well, ask your partner the following questions and write down their answers for them. They will then do the same for you.
   - What was the event you organised?
   - What did you want to happen?
   - Was there something like it that you had organised in the past? If so, what?
   - Was this previous event successful?
   - How did you know whether it had been successful? – You should think of at least five points.

   1. _____
   2. _____
   3. _____
   4. _____
   5. _____

   - How did you know this current event had been successful?

   1. _____
   2. _____
   3. _____
   4. _____
   5. _____

   - What did you do to make sure that all those points of success were achieved?

   1. _____
   2. _____
   3. _____
   4. _____
   5. _____

Logical problem solver

You are 'Hot' at:

- Finding things to be logical about
- Thinking about things
- Looking for the way things work
- Analysing the people you deal with

Your task, should you wish to accept it, is:

1. Think of a time when you had a problem to solve. It might have been something at school, at home or with friends.

2. Working with your partner, go through the activity sheet asking them the questions and writing down the answers for them. They will then do the same for you.
   - What was the problem?
   - When you looked at the problem, what did you:
     – See?
     – Hear?
     – Feel?
   - Instead of the problem, what did you want to:
     – See?
     – Hear?
     – Feel?
   - Was there something like it that you had solved in the past? If so, what?
   - Was this past problem successfully resolved?
   - How did you know? – Think of at least five things that showed you it was successful in the end.

     1. _____
     2. _____
     3. _____
     4. _____
     5. _____

   - How would you know that this current problem had been successfully solved?

     1. _____
     2. _____
     3. _____
     4. _____
     5. _____

   - What did you do to make sure that all these points of success were achieved?

     1. _____
     2. _____
     3. _____
     4. _____
     5. _____

Team-building problem solver

You are 'Hot' at:

- Working with other people
- Being aware that how you feel has an effect on how well you do something
- Seeing that one thing is a part of something bigger
- Learning from other experiences you have had
- Getting information visually

Your task, should you wish to accept it, is:

1. Think of a time when you had a problem to solve. It might have been something at school, at home or with friends.
    Working with your partner, go through the activity sheet asking them the questions and writing down the answers for them. They will then do the same for you.

    - What was the problem?
    - When you looked at the problem what did you:
      – See?
      – Hear?
      – Feel?
    - Instead of the problem, what did you want to:
      – See?
      – Hear?
      – Feel?
    - Was there something like it that you had solved in the past? If so, what?
    - Was this past problem successfully resolved?
    - How did you know? – Think of at least five things that showed you that it was successful in the end.

      1. _____
      2. _____
      3. _____
      4. _____
      5. _____

    - How would you know that this current problem had been solved?

      1. _____
      2. _____
      3. _____
      4. _____
      5. _____

- What did you do to make sure that all these points had been successfully achieved?

    1. _____
    2. _____
    3. _____
    4. _____
    5. _____

Skilled problem solver

You are 'Hot' at:

- Using lots of different skills
- Solving problems
- Keeping things to time
- Changing things
- Finding people to help you

1. Think of a problem that you have solved in the past. It might be something at school, at home or with friends.
2. Working with your partner, go through the activity sheet, asking them the questions and writing down their answers for them. They will then do the same for you.

    - What was the problem?
    - When you looked at the problem what did you:
      – See?
      – Hear?
      – Feel?
    - Instead of the problem, what did you want to:
      – See?
      – Hear?
      – Feel?
    - Was there something like it that you had solved in the past? If so, what?
    - Was this past problem successfully resolved?
    - How did you know? – Think of at least five things that showed you that it was successful in the end.

    1. _____
    2. _____
    3. _____
    4. _____
    5. _____

- How would you know that this current problem had been solved?

  1. _____
  2. _____
  3. _____
  4. _____
  5: _____

- What did you do to make sure that all these points had been successfully achieved?

  1. _____
  2. _____
  3. _____
  4. _____
  5. _____

How we take in information and how we use it will help students use learning strategies that work for them and empower staff to mediate effectively in a student's learning.

Learning Strategy

Your learning style describes your preference to learn either visually, aurally or kinaesthetically, your thinking style describes how you deal with the information you have received and your learning strategy describes how you achieve a certain outcome.

You may have a preferred learning style, and a particular thinking style, but strategies are learnt and can be developed and changed with the appropriate interventions. By changing the strategy you employ, you can have a great impact on the outcome. For example, most good spellers spell visually. They can see a wrongly spelled word on a page very quickly. It jumps out at them. Poor spellers often are auditory learners and overuse phonics as a spelling method. By changing the strategy and teaching a poor speller to use more visual strategies, such as the technique of visualisation, they will have a strategy that works. There follows a spelling exercise that you may find interesting.

Activity sheet: Visualisation and specific skills
Spelling strategy
The students have 30 seconds to memorise the following words. They can do it however they want, though they should remember the strategy they use.

leucocytes (white blood corpuscles)

chrysanthemum
pyrotechnics

After 30 seconds they should try to write the words. They get a mark for every letter they get right and lose a mark for every letter that should have been there but wasn't. Letters that are wrong are ignored. Add up their score.

In their pairs they should share their strategy with their partner. How did you do that?

Take another word that they are unfamiliar with, and is fairly long, e.g. quagmire. Write the word of your choice so that all the children can see it. Ask them to work in pairs, one as learner and one as mentor, and follow these instructions:

1. Look at the word and then move their eyes so that they are looking up and to the left, so that they can visualise the word. They can either close their eyes, which may be easier, or keep their eyes open.
2. If they are having trouble visualising, it may be because they do not normally use visual strategies. Suggest they visualise something they are very familiar with, for example their front door, and then try to visualise the word on their front door.
3. The learner should then spell the word to the mentor. When they are successful they should look at the word on the board, look away and to the left and up, and visualise it again. This time they should spell the word backwards to their mentor.
4. They should now use this technique on the following words, taking it in turns to be learner and mentor:

    tagliatelle
    nitrogenous
    bourgeois

Helpful hints
*   Picture the words in your favourite colour.
*   Make any unclear letters stand out by making them different in some way, e.g. bigger, brighter.
*   Break the word into groups of three letters, and build the word up in these blocks.
*   Put the letters on a familiar background.
*   If it is a long word, make the letters small enough so that you can see the whole word.
*   Trace the letters in the air with your finger as you picture them in your mind.
*   The words are those above, or any of your choice that have the same number of letters.

Score your success this time and compare with your first go at spelling. Find out how many students improved their score, how many did the same and how many did worse.

Learning strategies are crucial to motivation and success in learning. All too often students get stuck in a routine of doing things the same way, whether they are working or not. They carry on banging their head against a door that opens the other way, become demotivated and receive advice that they should work harder.

When students have become aware of how they learn and are developing strategies to improve their performance, it can be a great time for them to start to use one another as a learning resource. Trust the students; they are fabulous learners and will be ready to share how they did something more readily than they will to share their outcomes because the process is less judgemental. There are always thousands of ways to do something, theirs was merely one. Outcomes are always considered in better or worse terms.

Levels of Learning

The third building block of learning is the different levels at which learning takes place. The levels start to bring the various building blocks of learning together. The levels of learning are:

- Environment – The 'when' and 'where' of learning.
- Behaviour – The 'what' of learning.
- Capability – The 'how' of learning.
- Belief – The 'why' of learning.
- Identity – The 'who' of learning.
- Spirituality – The context of learning.

Environment

Creating an environment where students can learn using the variety of learning and thinking styles is critically important and has largely been described in the 'Sequence of Learning' section of this chapter.

Behaviour

Behaviour in the levels of learning is in part about control and order. It is impossible to learn if there is chaos around. It is, however, just as important as any other learning strategy and involves the physiology of learning and learning styles.

Capability

Explores 'how' you learn. Having the skills to employ a range of learning strategies that will help you achieve your goals

Belief

It is when we start to consider the issues of belief in learning that we rediscover, in its purest form, the power of emotional intelligence. What we believe, about ourselves, other people, the world around us, will determine what we feel. If I believe that the world is a threatening place full of danger, then I will feel anxiety and stress. If I believe that other people are selfish and not to be trusted then I will feel very defensive. If I believe that I am not a very worthy person and do not deserve success, then I may feel inhibited. All these are simple, though common, examples of limiting beliefs. Developing emotional intelligence empowers people to challenge those beliefs that they find are limiting their learning, their success in life and ultimately their happiness. Self-awareness is the starting point of change and once this is developed, it is then possible for students to learn to be more optimistic, have more empathy, be ambitious for themselves, and have integrity and congruence in what they do.

Empowering people to change their beliefs is remarkably straightforward, tremendously effective and can open children's minds to the power of their own ability to learn. Part of this can be done in a normal PSHE lesson and part of it can be done in the interactions staff can have with individuals and groups. Emotional intelligence must not be seen as just part of the curriculum, it has to be lived as well. An example of a belief-changing activity is 'The Circle of Excellence' which students will work with really well and derive great benefit from. The skill is partly in the activity itself and partly from knowing when to use it. Pacing in learning is crucial and a central thread of the emotional learning programme.

Circle of success

- Create circles of learning and circles of success on the floor.

- Step into your circle of learning and see what you see, hear what you hear and feel what you feel as a learner today.
- Step out of the circle and shake those feelings off.
- Step into the circle of success and remember a time when you were a fabulous and successful learner; see what you saw, hear what you heard and feel what you felt then.
- Step out of the circle and shake off those feelings.
- Step into the circle of learning and bring over to you from the circle of success those resources you need to be the fabulous learner you are. See what you see, hear what you hear and feel what you feel.

- Create an anchor for those feelings so that you can recall them whenever you need them.
- When you are ready, you may come back.

The following activity helps students to identify and analyse the emotions that enable others to be successful.

Activity sheet: Learning success from others

1. Get into groups of three.
2. Divide your A1 sheet of paper into six and write the names of six people who you think are successful. They may be sports people, people in politics, musicians, or someone you know. It doesn't matter whether anyone else knows who they are.
3. Draw a picture or diagram or symbol that represents each person and what they have that makes them successful.
4. Swap your paper with another group and write against the diagram, symbol or picture the emotions you think someone would feel if they were described in the way the other group have described them.
5. Join the other group and write down in your Learning Journal all the emotions that have been written down.
6. See if you can group them together in some way. What is the emotion that describes the group of words you have?
7. Group the feedback about the emotions for success.
8. List all the emotions that have been described and group them. What now are your emotions for success?
9. Take each of the emotions and remember a time when you have felt that feeling.
10. Describe that time in your Learning Journal.
11. Create an emotional memory for each of those feelings.

Creating emotional intelligence in the curriculum is essential if we are really going to have an impact on giving students an understanding of their potential. It is equally crucial that the work continues with the day-to-day exchanges between students and staff. I have covered below an example of an experience I had whilst Head of a school.

A 14-year-old boy was brought to my office because he was continually disturbing lessons with violent outbursts. He came with his grandmother who clearly had temper problems of her own. After 20 minutes of establishing a shared view of the basic facts and the consequences if there were further outbursts, I began to try to work with the boy to establish what he could do to avoid the problem erupting again. After some initial discussion I asked him how he felt just before he hit another child. The rest of the discussion was as follows:

Student: "I don't know, I just feel funny."

It was obvious that he didn't have the vocabulary to allow this line to go much further, but I was aware that he was visualising his feelings.

Me: "Can you see the feeling?"
Student: "Yes."

He looked up and to the left and then down at the desk we were sitting alongside.

Me: "What does it look like?"
Student: "It's sort of round and white and pulsing."
Me: "How big is it?"
Student: "About the size of a football."
Me: "Can you make it stop pulsing?"
Student: "Yes."

He didn't move his eyes off the desktop and was clearly real about what he was saying.

Me: "How big is it?"
Student: "Still a football."
Me: "Can you make it smaller?"
Student: "Yes."
Me: "How big is it now?"

He showed me with his hands something that was smaller than a football. We repeated the question and answers about reducing the size of the feeling twice more.

Me: "And now what does the feeling look like?"
Student: " Oh, it's just big and white."
Me: "And how do you feel about that?"
Student: "Oh, that's OK."
Me: "And what will happen when you get that feeling again?"
Student: "That's no problem, I'll think of that (*he points to the desk top*), I can handle that."

I have summarised the dialogue slightly, though the whole exchange took only about ten minutes. The student left my office with a belief that he could control his temper and had the skills to allow him to do it.

Belief change is the central feature of working with emotional intelligence: taking away from young people the belief that they cannot achieve something, and giving them the personal ambition and motivation to become the very best they can.

Identity

The question 'who' applies to identity and learning. The ultimate goal of learning in school is to have the students see themselves as lifelong learners engaged in a continual process of personal growth and development, taking every opportunity to learn. A year 8 student on a training programme I ran had completed the task of drawing a metaphor of learning. He had to describe through the metaphor where he saw himself now and where he would like to be in the future. He drew a series of hurdles with a figure standing in between them. In describing his metaphor, he said that as we grow older the difficulties confronting us grow. However, if we continue to grow then the problems will actually remain the same size. The question of learning at the level of identity is the goal of developing emotional intelligence in schools, to allow children to use their experiences at school to fast-track them as lifelong learners.

Spirituality

This is the moral and ethical domain of learning. It is about developing the personal integrity that will direct your learning. Not all learning is congruent with someone's personal beliefs and values. It should not be OK to disrupt the learning of others, learn to be a great burglar or believe that violence is a solution. Behaviour in these areas will emerge from the success of an EQ programme as students develop emotionally and are able to make decisions based on their own sense of self in the wider world.

The structure of learning provides the capability to work at the level of belief, which is one major factor in determining our feelings and emotions. The next chapter will take a closer look at what our emotions are and the part the brain plays in determining our emotional state and how it ensures the supremacy of emotion over intellect.

Chapter Two
Emotions and Learning

"Learning takes up no time at all, it is not learning that takes the time"
Marshall Thurber
Attorney, businessman, educationalist

Understanding emotional intelligence and realising what can be done to develop it in the classroom is based on the exploration of certain fundamental questions. These need to be answered in the context of our understanding of the way the brain works as an emotional organ.

- What are emotions?
- What is the difference between emotions and feelings?
- Can we really control our emotional state?
- Can we create the right emotions when we need them?

The Emotional Brain

The impact of emotion on how the brain works is best understood by looking at the mechanics of brain function. In doing this we will be examining the neurological basis for learning styles and strategy, thinking styles and memory. We will be describing the very relationship between the brain and emotional intelligence.

The Neuron

The capacity of each individual to learn is staggering almost beyond belief and, contrary to popular myth, many aspects of brain function, particularly those affecting EQ, can improve with age. In the brain alone, there are between 10,000,000,000 and 100,000,000,000 neural cells or neurons. This means that the minimum number of potential thought patterns of the average brain is 1 followed by 10.5 kilometres of typewritten zeros. As a result, the average brain can learn seven facts per second, every second, for the rest of your life and still have room for more.

Few people's learning is limited to the point of their current achievement by the capacity of their brain. Their achievement is limited by how they believe they can use what they have, and this can change.

The neurons of the brain are the building blocks of how the brain works. How they are arranged and how they react with other neurons is also the key to understanding the difference between IQ and EQ. The neurons look rather like a tree. The roots are called dendrites and the trunk the axon. The branches of the tree are the axon terminals.

Stimulation is received through our senses and our preferred learning style and then transmitted by the dendrites through the cell body. If enough stimulation reaches the cell body then it fires an 'action potential' along its axon to the axon terminals. These in turn form synapses onto the dendrites of neighbouring neurons. Each neuron in the cortex of the brain has between 1000 and 10,000 synapses communicating with neighbouring neurons. The power of learning lies in these neural connections that are made in the brain.

Repeated stimulation causes the synapses to be fired and neural pathways to be laid down. This is why repetition is so important in learning. It is why rote learning does work up to a point. The point at which it stops working, of course, is when the students fall asleep through all-consuming boredom. Repetition, though, is important to learning and memory. The more often the stimulation is received then the more often the synapse fires and the thicker and more substantial the connections become, and the deeper and more permanent is the learning.

There is a direct relationship between how we structure our lessons and the way the brain works.

- Students need to be ready to learn – relaxed and receptive to the stimulation of their learning environment.
- Stimulation should be multi-sensory – giving students the chance to use their preferred learning style.
- Feedback should be immediate, specific and reinforce learning.
- Learning should be continually reviewed and concerned with how the learning is taking place, the learning strategy and the success of learning.
- Learning should be mediated through 'How' questions.
- Each lesson should contain several starts and finishes.
- Provide choice – not in 'what' is learnt but in 'how' it is learnt.

The structure of our lessons will create the thinking that leads to learning. How we think, our preferred style, is a consequence of the brain being able to think in different ways. These are serial thinking (IQ), associative thinking (EQ) and unitive thinking (co-operation between EQ and IQ).

Neural Intelligence, Serial Thinking and the Brain's IQ

The wiring of the brain varies to support the different types of thinking it is designed to perform. Serial thinking, the type measured in IQ, is supported by neural tracts that are linked in series. Each one is dependent on the neurons on either side of it to function properly, somewhat like a rather old set of Christmas tree lights. They are fine whilst all the bulbs work, but when one fails the whole string stops working. The same applies to serial thinking in the brain.

Serial thinking operates to a fixed programme, which means that there can be little learning or development in this area. What you are given is what you've got. To say our capacity to think in a rational and logical way is limited by what we inherit may be correct. To say that we are using what we have to its fullest potential is something very different.

Because of the mutual dependency of the neurons in this sort of arrangement there has until recently been a common view that brain function reduces with age. This is clearly evident in observing the gentle deterioration in our ability to remember as we grow older. This assumption is now being powerfully challenged. The two main tenets of the argument are, firstly, that this is a matter of perception and not fact, and, secondly, it just isn't true! We perceive our abilities with memory in an interesting and somewhat self-deprecating way. If my eight-year-old son is at the height of his powers of memory then I doubt there is any hope for him or many of his peers. Lunch boxes left in the fridge, jumpers at school, books lost. He inhabits a haphazard world where his sense of Gestalt seems to be totally lacking, and if his memory is to begin to decline in the none-too-distant future then it seems there is little chance of redemption. But does he care? His 49-year-old father on the other hand, with considerably fewer brain cells, remembers slightly more (sometimes a matter of dispute) but is more inclined to beat himself up a little for forgetting. To some degree, memory loss is a matter of perception and not a factor of age.

More powerfully, there is increasing evidence that declining mental capacity as a factor of age is not to do with reduced ability but with reduced use. If you train your brain in the way that some choose to train their muscles and develop memory techniques as a natural part of your world, then not only will there be no diminution in capability, but capability will improve with the repetition of practice brought about as we mature.

Give children new strategies for learning and their achievement will continue to grow. Give them the belief that they are all fabulous learners and their learning will continue to grow throughout their lives.

Experiential Intelligence, Associative Thinking and the Brain's EQ

This is thinking that enables us to make associations between different types of stimulation and then develop intelligent and supportive behaviour. It is the core of the emotional brain and the powerhouse of thinking, memory and emotion.

The difference in the way the brain works is that you are now using bundles of neurons, with each neuron acting upon many others all at the same time. These neural bundles have the ability to rewire themselves in the light of experience. Learning changes the strengths between connections and, as neural elements fire together, their connections become stronger. Associative thinking is centred in the limbic system of the brain, which is its emotional centre. It is here, through experiential learning, that emotion is the driving force of brain function.

> "The only kind of learning which significantly influences behaviour is self-discovered learning – truth that has been assimilated in experience"
>
> Carl Rogers

The development of emotional associations is generally slow, though very persuasive and powerful, and reflects the movement from feeling to emotion. A child's feeling towards a particular subject or their belief in their ability to learn is gradually formed and has a profound effect on their feelings towards school and their willingness to learn.

Emotional Memory

Memory is a simple question of associating something you want to remember with something that is either:

- commonplace, such as a number, letter or place;
- enjoyable for you, for example sport, sex, the seaside;
- fantastic, full of colour, the absurd, contradictions and emotion.

The paradox of memory is that its power and simplicity are hidden from view by its very power and simplicity. Memory works through association; all too often memory is associated with inherited intelligence and therefore it is assumed that it cannot be learnt. Little attention is then paid in school to improving a child's memory. That association lowers expectation, in some cases removing it totally, and stops us learning and helping others to learn what fabulous memories we all have.

Learning to have a fabulous memory is merely learning to associate what you want to learn with a particular learning style, either visual, auditory or kinaesthetic. The second stage is to be able to associate what you want to remember with more than one learning style and then, most powerfully, to add emotion.

Examples of activities that will pace this learning are described below.

Activity Sheet: Introducing Memory

The purpose of this activity is to begin to explore the ways in which we remember:

- how you best remember;
- how you can begin to use the fabulous memory you have when you need it.

Firstly, fill in the memory sheets below, putting any sequence of numbers and letters on the top line of each sheet.

Work in threes, where one is the 'teacher', one the 'learner' and one the 'observer'. You will all have a go at each of the roles.

Visual memory
1. Start with the visual sheet. The person who is the teacher holds up their list of numbers and letters for the learner to remember. You have 30 seconds, which will be timed by the observer.
2. At the end of 30 seconds the learner points to the letters and numbers in the sequence that they remember them and the teacher writes them down.
3. The teacher asks the learner if they can say what they did to try to remember the sequence of letters and numbers. The teacher should make some notes on the score sheet.
4. Fill in the boxes showing the number the learner got right and the number that were out of order.
5. Change roles and do the exercise again, so that everyone has a turn as teacher, learner and observer.
6. Look at the notes and see if there is anything that you learn from one another about remembering visually.
7. Take the ones you think are best and write them on the board or paper your teacher has put up.
8. Write the ones that you want to try into your Learning Journal.

Hot tips on visual memory
*   Be aware of what you are doing to get ready for remembering.
*   Look up and to the left to see what you need to remember clearly. If you are left-handed, try up and to the right.
*   Break long sequences into manageable chunks of maybe three or four characters.
*   It is OK to get some of them wrong.

Auditory memory
This is the same exercise, though this time it is all done through speaking.

1. The teacher reads out 10 random letters and numbers.
2. The learner listens and can ask for the sequence to be repeated up to three times. You can ask for the list to be read a little faster or slower if you want.
3. If the learner has remembered the sequence before the third hearing then they can have a go. They should say what they believe the sequence to be and the teacher should fill in the check sheet and ask the learner what they were doing to try to remember the letters and numbers.
4. This is repeated so that everyone gets a go.

5. Read the notes you have gathered and write the ones you think are best on the board or on the paper the teacher has provided, so that everybody can see.
6. Write the ones you want to try into your Learning Journal.
7. Do the auditory memory exercise a second time, using new strategies.

Hot tips on auditory memory
*   Be aware of what you are doing to get ready for remembering.
*   Try to tune in the voice of the person who is speaking so that you can hear it really clearly.
*   Are you remembering the sound or are you trying to turn the sound into a visual picture?
*   It is OK to get some of them wrong.

Kinaesthetic memory
The exercise in threes is repeated with the roles moving around.

1. The sequence of letters and numbers is described to the learner by the teacher physically by:

    *   Taking the learner's hand and tracing the letters and numbers in the air
    *   Taking the learner's hand and tracing the letters and numbers on the desk with their finger
    *   Drawing the letters and numbers on the palm of the learner's hand.
    *   Drawing the letters and numbers on the learner's back; as they do so, the learner writes them on their own palm.

    The sequence can be repeated up to three times.

2. When the learner is ready they write down the sequence they have remembered and the teacher records it on their check sheet
3. Describe what you were doing to learn kinaesthetically and make notes on the check sheet.
4. Share your learning strategies. Take them to the front and record them on the board or on the paper your teacher has provided.
5. Write down the ones you would like to try in your Learning Journal.
6. Go through the kinaesthetic exercise a second time, trying new strategies for remembering.
7. Record your score.

Hot tips for kinaesthetic learning
*   Be aware of what you do to be ready to remember.
*   Are you picturing the shapes, giving them a sound or a feeling?
*   You can get some of them wrong.

Hot Tips for Emotional Memory

- The more ways you can use to receive, store and retrieve memory, the more you will increase your success.
- When you are trying to remember something, remember where you were when you learned it. Seeing yourself back in that time and place will help you to remember what you need.
- Use stories to remember; seeing, hearing and feeling the story.
- Develop specific strategies for things you will need to remember, using sights, sounds and feelings.
- Remembering names: See someone new that you meet with their name printed on their forehead.
- Spelling: Look up and to the left and see the word so that you can spell it forwards and backwards.
- Sequences: Make them into a story by associating them with something else that you really enjoy. Let your imagination run riot! The more extreme you make the story and the association, the more likely you are to remember it.

Associative thinking is the way in which much emotional learning will take place. It is also the basis of all memory models. Memory is developed by associating one thing with another: putting a name to a face, seeing a pram and suddenly remembering that you have left your baby outside the post office (as my mother did!). Sometimes we are not sure what association suddenly prompts a thought or memory, those moments of *déjà vu* that often remain unexplained at a conscious level.

The centre of emotional memory in the brain is the amygdala. Here there are neurological links between the amygdala and the neocortex, allowing moments of emotional dominance when feelings rapidly override rational or sequential thinking. The power of emotion will often come from an emotional memory, an association of a current situation with a past event. Success lies in retrieving positive memories, which we can all have access to, and discarding negative memories that are often seen as negative because of the power we invest in others to tell us whether we have been a success or not.

The emotional memory is extremely powerful and can bring back memories as strong as the initial event. Chemically, the adrenal gland hormones, epinephrine and noreinephrine, are present both in the emotion of an event and in the recall of the memory. That very power highlights the need to develop emotional learning as part of our classroom practice. Understanding our emotional memory gives us access to emotional emancipation and empowerment in our learning and life.

Co-operation Between IQ and EQ – Unitive Thinking

It would be wrong to suggest that in different circumstances people think in either a serial or an associated way, with the two processes acting independently.

There is integration between the two, which is essential if we are going to achieve all that we can. One example of this is the research done by Seymour and Norwood in 1993 into the thinking of chess players. They found that good players used both types of thinking when they were confronted with common positions you might expect to find in a chess game. The good player didn't laboriously search every option using serial thinking but used a combination of the two to find solutions. Poor players would break positions down and seek to find solutions, having tested the possible implications of moving individual pieces. When the two groups were confronted by situations that were random and for which neither had recourse to associative thinking, they fared equally badly. Success in chess and in other problem-solving activities is made more likely with the use of both serial and associated thinking.

Emotional intelligence is the ability to control and use the power of our emotions to maximise our potential and personal effectiveness. Our emotional intelligence has been learnt. We are not *born* optimistic or with high self-esteem, but we learn it through experience and association until it becomes our 'second' nature. That no one is responsible for me other than me, and that I can make a great me, is not always acknowledged. There is a lovely cartoon with a couple sitting on a park bench; the man turns to his partner and says "You know, you are right, Priscilla, I do tend to blame others. I must have inherited it from my parents."

The questions I raised at the start of this chapter can now be considered in the light of our understanding of the role of the brain as an emotional organ:

- What are emotions?
- What is the difference between emotions and feelings?
- Can we really control our emotional state?
- Can we create the right emotions when we need them?

What are Emotions?

There have been several attempts to categorise and define emotions in some form. The most concentrated study was that by Paul Ekman and Wallace Friesen of the University of California who, in their book *Unmasking the Face*, sought to discover if there were basic emotions common to different cultures throughout the world. This is important because, if the study suggests that some emotions are common to every human being and every culture, the inference is that they may be out of our conscious or even subconscious control. They may be as solid and immovable a part of the human condition as sleep, hunger, thirst and death and, if so, what of the future for emotional intelligence? Their study concluded that all societies recognise:

- fear;
- anger;
- sadness;
- enjoyment.

It would seem that whatever we choose to do, at some point in our lives we are going to have these emotions. But does this invalidate the view that emotions are within our orbit of conscious influence and can be learnt?

Daniel Goleman, in *Emotional Intelligence*, developed emotional categories and added love, surprise, disgust and shame. He then added subsets of each of these, where I am sure all of us could add our own subdivisions and feel empathy towards the words we chose.

Emotions bridge thought, feeling and action – they operate in every part of a person, affecting and being affected by emotion.

What is the Difference Between Emotions and Feelings?

There are, then, emotions that we are all destined to feel as part of the human condition. What, though, are the differences between emotions and feelings?

Emotions are imprinted and recurring feelings sustained by a belief, as a response to which we take some form of action. If I feel scared in a dark wood it is a feeling I have at that time. If I learn to believe that all dark woods are threatening and feel fear every time I go into one, then I have an imprinted emotion about dark woods. The derivation of the word emotion comes from the Latin root '*movere*' to move. Part of our understanding of emotion and emotional intelligence is that there are behaviours that are associated with our emotions. The purpose of developing emotional intelligence is partly to give control over our emotions and partly to give us the personal authority to decide how we act in response to them.

The importance of distinguishing between feelings and emotions in school is to realise how much schools do to turn the feelings children have, about themselves and learning, into beliefs and emotions that then dominate the child's behaviour. We know that not all that behaviour is positive.

There will be few people reading this book who won't have a subject in the school curriculum that they feel they are not very good at, or who feel frustrated that they didn't do as well in a subject as they should have. Associative thinking has been at play. Without doubt you would have associated that subject with something or someone that created inhibiting feelings that were reinforced until you believed them. Ask any group of 12 adults who of them cannot sing and 6 will put their hands up. Subjects of the National Curriculum are rarely emotional vessels themselves, but become them when they are associated with something else: "I love French", "I hate Maths". Find the association people have with their inhibitions to learn and you empower people to become the very best they can be at the whole of the curriculum.

Associative thinking is a powerful process and helps create our emotional memory, which has a profound effect on what we believe and how we behave. We can, however, learn to change our emotional memory if it is not helping our learning. It will not change the experience, though we can change the perceptions we have of that experience. We can then reframe the beliefs in our inability to achieve in a way that will support learning and not inhibit it.

One section of the Magic Learning Programme is called 'My best subject is...'. I have reproduced it below to illustrate how self-imposed blocks to learning can be removed. They draw on a variety of learning and thinking styles.

It is possible to try the activities with students without preparation, though they would normally form a relatively advanced part of the programme. The students would then already be used to working with visualisation and sharing learning experiences.

My best subject is...

The class should be in groups of three:

- *The teacher*
- *The student*
- *The observer*

Agree a lesson that you will use for this exercise.

Agree 5 activities that you might engage in during lessons in this subject. They could include listening, reading, answering questions and so on.

The teacher names at random an activity. The student has to portray someone through mime, who is not succeeding during this section of the lesson. The observer has to write down what emotions they think lie behind the behaviour.

The observer checks with the student what they saw and what emotions they may have been feeling.

The observer records what is said in their Learning Journal.

Change roles so that everyone has a go and until each of the activities of the lesson has been covered.

Now repeat the activity with a different lesson and a student who is succeeding in each of the activities of the lesson.

Record in your journals a list of behaviours of success, and the emotions that lie underneath them.

Vroooooooooming behaviour

Work in pairs.

1. *Think of something you want to change. An activity that happens in one lesson, or perhaps in several.*
2. *Student A asks student B: "Have you thought of an activity?"*
3. *If yes, carry on. If no, student A suggests B choose something from the list they looked at in the 'My best subject is…' exercise.*
4. *Student A asks B to create a picture on their screen of themselves during this activity.*
5. *Look at the picture and adjust it in the following ways. If when you change it you feel good, then keep it, if not then return it to how it was:*
   - *Increase the brightness.*
   - *Make your picture closer, and then further away.*
   - *Make your picture bigger and then smaller.*
   - *Make your picture more colourful.*
   - *Make your picture clearer.*
   - *Make your picture move.*
6. *Step into your picture so that you can see yourself in the situation you want to change.*
7. *Create a new dark picture of what you want to be, in this situation you want to change, in the bottom left-hand corner of your picture.*
8. *At the same time, shrink the old picture and expand the new one as quickly as you can, saying vrrroooooom to yourself as the new picture rapidly grows.*
9. *Repeat this 10 times.*
10. *Change roles.*

When you are at home at the end of the day you may want to try the Vrrrooooooom exercise in your Learning Journal.

Walk the learner's walk

How would you walk if you were really ready to learn?

1. *The teacher asks for a volunteer.*
2. *Walk alongside the volunteer, matching what they are doing.*
3. *As you match the angle of their head, their field of vision, their breathing, sense how it feels for you and then make suggestions to the volunteer. These should be simple, specific and sympathetic, e.g. "Look straight ahead", " Relax your shoulders", "Slow your stride".*
4. *Ask the group if they have any they might add.*
5. *Find a partner and practise 'the learner's walk'.*
6. *Group feedback.*

My best subject is … (2)

Work with a partner.

Student A asks student B the following questions and writes down the answers in their partner's Learning Journal.

1. *Which is the subject where you are least successful?*
2. *How do you know you are least successful in this subject?*
3. *Remember a lesson in this subject when you were unsuccessful. Put up your video screen and feel comfortable so that you can see the screen clearly. Remember the lesson when you were unsuccessful and see yourself on your video screen. Tell your partner what you:*
    *   *See*
    *   *Hear*
    *   *Do*
4. *In the lesson that tells you that you were being unsuccessful:*
    *   *How did you feel during the lesson?*
    *   *Did your feelings change?*
    *   *What happened that made them change?*
    *   *What can you learn from knowing that your feelings changed during the lesson?*
5. *Which is the subject where you are most successful?*
6. *How do you know you are most successful in this subject?*
7. *Remember a lesson in this subject when you were successful. Put up your video screen and feel comfortable so that you can see the screen clearly. Remember the lesson when you were successful and see yourself on your video screen. Tell your partner what you:*
    *   *See*
    *   *Hear*
    *   *Do*
8. *In the lesson that tells you that you were being successful:*
    *   *How did you feel during the lesson?*
    *   *Did your feelings change?*
    *   *What happened that made them change?*
    *   *What can you learn from knowing that your feelings changed during the lesson?*
9. *Put up a split screen so that you can see both lessons and you in each. Take the you in the successful lesson and watch yourself walk into your unsuccessful lesson.*
10. *What resources do you take with you into your unsuccessful lesson that you can give to the you there?*
11. *Give the you in this unsuccessful lesson the resources you need to succeed.*
12. *What will you do when you are in your next lesson in your least successful subject?*

Associative thinking is the central feature of our learning. When those associations have emotions woven into them, there is the basis of lasting change and lifelong learning. Emotional association allows the student to bridge their learning in one environment to another; from the classroom to the home or the park or disco, the emotion remains constant: driving, enabling or constraining learning in whatever environment you may want to use it. Emotional association is also the cornerstone of memory.

Schools work very hard to try to change negative behaviour, though they usually fail. They fail not because of lack of effort, determination or commitment, but because they are trying to change the wrong thing. If we go back to the levels of learning, we start to realise that behaviour is a consequence of belief and capability. At any point in time, the students are doing what they believe they are capable of, and their behaviour reflects those beliefs in relation to their perception of the environment of school.

Feelings are temporary, though unless the environment within schools is optimistic, positive, constructive and welcoming, the school will work to turn those feelings a child has into negative beliefs. Emotional intelligence needs to be lived if it is to have the impact of which it is capable; it needs to be in the whole environment of school, and in its very fabric. The late Cardinal Bernardin in Chicago used to say: " Preach the Gospel every day, and, if necessary, use words."

Can we Control our Emotional State?

There are two levels at which emotional intelligence works and provides us with such power in our lives. Ekman and Goleman are dealing with the first. Some emotions are inevitable and healthy. They may also be temporarily painful and inhibiting as well. To feel grief at a friend's funeral, fear at the sight of an oncoming car, joy as we watch our children play, are all emotions that for the sake of safety and emotional balance we will feel.

What is *not* healthy and what we *can* learn to control is how long and when we feel these emotions. The grief of the loss of a friend does not have to stay with us every day and dominate our lives. If it does, we are still exercising choice and our emotional control, though in a way that has a negative impact on our ability to learn and enjoy life. This does not, however, mean that the person overburdened with grief or any other emotion must simply 'pull himself together'.

Underpinning the belief in emotional intelligence is the realisation that at any point in our lives we are just doing the very best we can with the personal emotional resources we have available to us. What emotional intelligence will do is to make people aware that they have more resources than they currently believe they have. They can choose to be continually dominated by the loss of a friend or relative, but it is a choice and not an inevitable consequence. We can choose it, no problem, but we need to be self-aware and realise, accept and own the consequences.

Emotional intelligence is not a sort of emotional fascism, "you will be happy and learn, because I know you can, … or else". Emotional intelligence is about empowerment; the realisation that you have control and can exercise it. However you choose to exercise your emotional control it will have consequences, which can be only your responsibility. You have to take responsibility for those consequences and accept they are yours and not dump them in the easy street of blame.

> "Whether you believe you can or whether you believe you can't you will probably be right"
>
> Henry Ford

It is worth pausing for a moment to reflect on what responsibility is. It is often seen as a heavy weight. People talk of the 'burden of responsibility', making it heavy, cold, static and inhibiting. It is in fact none of these things. Responsibility is a dynamic opportunity to be in control. It is, quite literally, the ability to respond. Becoming more emotionally intelligent is being empowered, having the capability and belief that you can take responsibility for your own learning and growth.

In school there will be children whom you don't reach and who continue to stick their tongues out at themselves and shout "I am dumb and you can't do anything about it" to any passer-by who they think might react. They will then find the evidence within their lives to support their belief. They will fail at school, in their social lives, in their jobs, all of which will be fuelling a belief that they have learnt. The tragedy is that they do have control and can learn to be the very best they can be, which for the vast majority of people is way beyond where they are at the moment.

Some emotions are part of the human condition, are painful and inhibiting, though they do not need to be everlasting, unless we choose to let them. Miss Haversham in Dickens' *Great Expectations* chose to have everlasting hate; there was another life she could have lived. Developing our emotional intelligence is empowering and puts each individual in control of the decisions they take by enabling them to create emotional states that allow intelligent decision making and intelligent behaviour.

Can we Create Emotions when we Need them?

Sustaining or limiting how we feel is one thing, but is it possible to create an emotional state at a point in time when it would best serve our needs? Going to the dentist, I may need courage but not feel it; to complete a task, I may need determination but feel disinterested; faced with a problem, I may need optimism but I am racked with pessimism.

It is possible, and easily so, to use our emotional memory to bring back emotions so that we have access to them when we need them. We do this naturally, though we tend to focus on the negative. Going to the dentist, I feel anxious because of my memories of previous experiences. My emotions about completing a task that I don't find very exciting are tainted by how I felt during similar tasks. Rather than letting the situation create the emotion, it can easily be reframed and turned around so that we are taking the right emotion to the situation. It is a similar difference to "I will believe it when I see it" being turned around to "I will see it when I believe it". The first is passive and the second is empowering and creative. Both work; it is merely a matter of choosing the one you want.

I have a bank of emotions that I have had in the past, which I can call on. I have been courageous (well, enough for the dentist), I have been determined, I have been optimistic. I can remember those emotions, bring them out from my memory and take them to the situation where I need them. This is a natural and powerful process and is described in the Magic Learning Programme in the anchoring strategies.

Emotions and Performance

Figure 2.1 shows how emotions affect performance.

Figure 2.1: How emotions affect performance

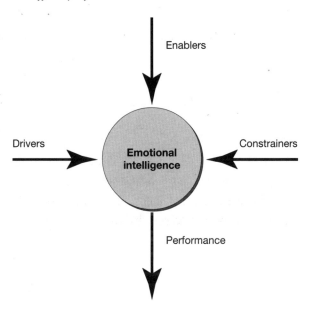

Enablers

These are emotions such as self-awareness, optimism, relaxation and self-esteem.

Drivers

These are emotions such as motivation, ambition, foresight and determination.

Constrainers

For example, integrity, pessimism, anxiety, fear and low self-esteem. Integrity may seem an odd one to have down, though not all learning will fit into someone's sense of personal identity and congruence. I would not want to learn to become a burglar or vandal.

Emotional Growth

The individual brain develops both cognitively and emotionally, being capable of different responses as its 'wearer' matures. Cognitively the brain develops to reflect Piaget's stages of child development. In a similar way, there are stages in a child's emotional development.

Erik Erikson suggested that there are eight stages of emotional growth and that if we are not successful in developing through one of the stages then there will be emotional immaturity and a limited emotional repertoire. Developing that repertoire is crucial to our development as learners. The importance of developing emotional intelligence in our schools is that where a stage of emotional growth has been missed or is limited, it can be returned to and successfully developed.

Age	Stages of Emotional Growth	Emotional Immaturity	Description
Prenatal to 1 year	Trust	Mistrust	Trust develops in response to the provision of basic needs. When the child is hungry it is fed, when wet, the child is changed and when it is cold it is made warm.
			The damage done by the child not developing this level of trust can lead to stunted physical as well as emotional development and can eventually lead to death. The condition is known as marasmus and has been well documented, particularly in orphans in war zones.
1–3 years	Autonomy	Dependency	Most parents will understand the wonders of this stage of a child's growth. You're late for work, it's raining, the cat needs feeding and is mewing around your ankles and your three-year-old is determined to put her own shoes on. Children take every opportunity to experiment with life and the possibilities that it offers.

Age	Stages of Emotional Growth	Emotional Immaturity	Description
3–6 years	Initiative	Guilt	This is a time of the developing imagination. A growing awareness of what can be is made even more wonderful by the imagination taking the possibilities to fantastic heights and depths. There are great games to be played, imaginary friends to share and sometimes blame when things go wrong. It is also a time for the development of fears as monsters emerge and children learn the power of imbuing spiders with dangerous qualities.
6–11 years	Industry	Inferiority	The child begins to develop a desire to be acknowledged, to be seen as being good at something. It is the development of a mind-set that starts to bridge competence from one place to another. If I am good at 'this', then maybe it's worth trying 'that', because I might be good at that too. Schools are not always as good as they can be at engaging this natural development. The Princes Trust reported in 1997 that "Young children have a repertoire of skills which they gradually learn not to use as they progress through school."
12–18 years	Identity	Role confusion	The difficulties and challenges of this stage of development are well documented and well known to parents and teachers alike. Some of the challenges are a natural part of maturation as we seek to be able to answer the questions about who we are and where we are going.
19–35 years	Intimacy	Isolation	Having created a sense of identity it is then possible to talk openly, honestly, disclosing our intimate thoughts and feelings without fear of rejection or of causing offence. Our relationships deepen and the direction our life takes is reflected by a sense of personal congruence and integrity.
36–60 years	Generative	Self-absorption	This is the ability to guide and coach, without a sense of personal payback being needed. The psychoanalyst Carl Rogers often referred to the need to be selfish before you can become selfless. We have to find ourselves before we can confirm what it is we can offer others.

(continued)

Age	Stages of Emotional Growth	Emotional Immaturity	Description
60+	Integrity	Despair	Although throughout our lives we would expect to find some of the emotional stages present, Erikson's stages in emotional development identify what will be dominating our development and learning at particular times in our lives. Integrity is something that you would hope and expect to find in most people to some degree throughout their lives. However, by their sixties most people will develop a sense of integrity of their lives with the wider world: a sense of order and purpose and perhaps a developing personal sense of God.

Our success as learners, in the classroom and in life, is determined by our success in using the power we have in emotional alchemy. Emotions will determine the destination we choose, the direction we take to reach that destination, and how far we travel towards our chosen goal.

Emotional intelligence will make us purposeful and successful learners. It is merely a question of bringing out what is within us.

Chapter Three
The Unlearned Lessons of Emotional Intelligence

"If there is not an inherent attracting power in the material, then…the teacher will either attempt to surround the material with foreign attractiveness, making a bid or offering a bribe for attention by 'making the lesson interesting'; or else will resort to…low marks, threats of non promotion, staying after school…But the attention thus gained…always remains dependent upon something external…True, reflective attention, on the other hand, always involves judging, reasoning, deliberation: it means that the child has a question of his own and is actively engaged in seeking and selecting relevant material with which to answer it."

John Dewey, 1915

A Brief History of Emotional Intelligence

Emotional intelligence is not new, neither is it a fad nor another coat of Emperor's clothes that appear to fit today though may not be visible tomorrow. Aristotle talked of emotional intelligence and I have no doubt that the literary-minded could find references before him and could chart the development of EQ through time.

> "Anyone can become angry – that is easy. But to be angry with the right person to the right degree, at the right time, for the right purpose, and in the right way – this is not easy"
>
> Aristotle
> Philosopher

More recently, the development of emotional intelligence moves side by side with the development of the affective education movement. The development of affective education is a history of misplaced opportunity. This perhaps is partly because the beliefs that underpin the progress of affective education were not fully understood; they were centred too much in the rather edgy world of psychoanalysis or were swamped by the tidal demands for education to be returned to its 'glorious past'. I shall trace the more recent developments in affective education in order that those misplaced opportunities can be rediscovered and applied to the development of emotional intelligence today.

Affective education has the student at its core. It is about what happens *within* the student, not what happens *to* the student. It is less about the experiences the student has than what they make of those experiences. If I get 5 out of 10 for my English essay I can believe either that it proves me right that I am no good at English, or that it is merely feedback from which I can learn. The experience is the same; the sense that is made of it is not. Affective education is a meta-process, reflecting on the learning of learning in the same way as the development of emotional intelligence today. The advantage is that today we have the benefit of a knowledge base of how the brain works that was denied to previous generations.

Affective Education

Figure 3.1: Affective education

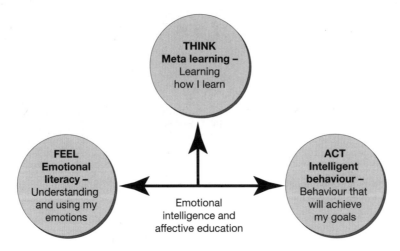

The history of affective education chronicles a journey through the motivation to learn, 'what' motivates people to learn, 'how' that motivation can be engaged and used, to the point of the learning process itself and how we learn. The role of the teacher in the process of learning is that of mediator and showing the students how they can model success by looking at their own success in similar areas, or model their success by looking at the achievements of others and understanding how they did that.

Thinking is best done when given a context and then the ability to keep the learning and add it to any new context that we find appropriate. The context of affective education and the development of emotional intelligence are wonderfully described through the concept of 'Invitational Education'.

Invitational Education

Invitational education is the context in which other developments of affective education sit. One of the strands of emotional intelligence is to give people awareness and control over the perceptions they have, to realise that how we see, hear and feel about something is determined in part by the environment we experience it in. That environment may be internal or external: how we see a meal when we are starving, or when it is a gourmet experience; a friend when we are lonely, or feeling good at a party; how we feel about our garden when it is well tended, or when we get back from a three-week break. In America in the 1970s an experiment was constructed where university students took on the role of prisoners and guards. The experiment had to be abandoned because both groups began to take on their role too deeply and see friends, not as they were, but as their role in the experiment. Change the environment and you begin to change the perception.

Invitational education becomes the contextual precursor of emotional intelligence. It is based on perceptual tradition and self-concept theory. What that means is that what we do is determined by how we see ourselves and the world we are in, and that each of us has a particular and individual view of that relationship. Go to a football match and see the variety of emotions that walk back out of the ground. Listen in the pubs on a Saturday night and you could believe that everyone had been to a different game. It is staggeringly true that a couple can go and see a film and discuss it afterwards. They have actually seen different films whilst sitting next to one another; if they had not, there would be nothing to say.

The five basic principles of invitational education are:

- People are able, valuable and responsible and should be treated accordingly if they are to develop fully.
- Learning is a collaborative act between student and student, and student and teacher. For this to happen, the relationship within the classroom has to serve that purpose. It has to be a relationship based on emotional understanding and rapport.
- Process is the product in the making. How we do something affects what we have in the end.
- People possess untapped positive potential in all areas of human endeavour.
- Potential can best be realised by places, policies, processes and programmes specifically designed to invite development.

Unlearned Lessons of Invitational Education – Summary

Invitational education offers the paradigm into which the other developments in affective education and emotional intelligence must fit. I was at a school that was about to be inspected. There was a sudden blossoming of signs around the school, in the three modern European languages that were taught and in Welsh as well as English. One student was heard to remark, while looking at the main entrance to the school, that the only sign he understood was the one that read, 'Students – No entry'.

Creating the environment for learning is crucially important in order that students see those opportunities in a positive way, and make the best use of them. It may be useful to examine your environment, classroom, department or school and see how it is supporting the learning needs of the students. You could do this by thinking about each of the 'levels of learning' in relation to the principles of invitational education.

Invitational Education Matrix

The questions that need to be asked in order to fill in the matrix (Figure 3.2) are:

Figure 3.2: Invitational education matrix

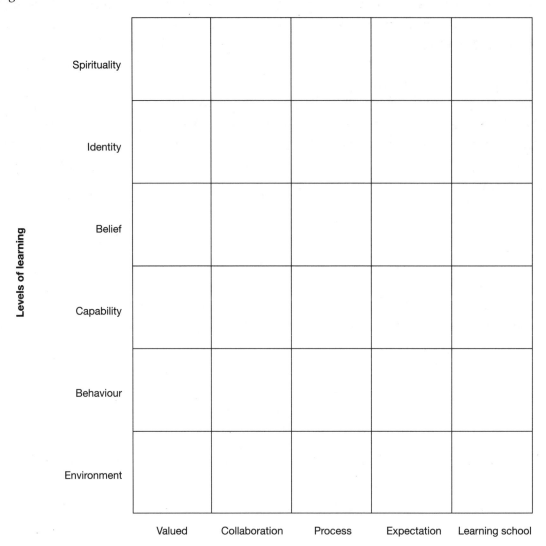

- In each of the levels of learning, what do you see, hear and feel that makes you believe that:
  1. the students are valued?
  2. there is collaborative learning?
  3. the process of learning is congruent with the school's aims and vision?
  4. the expectations reflect the potential of the students?
  5. the school, department or classroom is focused on learning?

It would be valuable to repeat the exercise and ask the same questions in a negative way and find out what is not congruent with the concept of invitational education.

- In each of the levels of learning, what do you see, hear and feel that makes you believe that:
  1. students are not valued?
  2. students are not learning in a collaborative environment?
  3. students are learning where the relationships are not congruent with the school's expressed aims and values?

4. students are not expected to achieve at a level that reflects their potential?
5. the central purpose of the activity is not learning?

Abraham Maslow

The recent development of affective education can be traced from the 1950s with Abraham Maslow's studies in peak performance. Maslow's major contribution was that he stopped researching failure and trying to solve it, and began to focus on success and how to replicate it.

He began to focus on what successful, happy people were doing, and what was motivating them to achieve their positive outcomes. To this end, Maslow was part of the school of content theorists who sought to answer the question, 'what' is it that motivates people?

> "People with high levels of personal mastery…cannot afford to choose between reason and intuition, or head and heart, any more than they would choose to walk on one leg or see with one eye"
>
> Peter Senge
> Author

Maslow maintained that basic personal need was only a motivator if it was unsatisfied. A person will only seek food when they are hungry, water when they are thirsty and warmth when they are cold. Each one of Maslow's hierarchy of human needs can only be met when the one below it has been satisfied. If I am feeling hungry then that is the focus of my attention, the focus of my consciousness, and I am not concerned with my friends, my personal esteem or how I might develop my capacity to learn. It may be worth considering Maslow's theories and reflecting on the availability of drinking water in school, the quality of school lunches, what happens to children on wet and cold days; reflecting on how well we are preparing children so that they can engage their natural, intrinsic desire to learn.

Maslow's hierarchy of human needs is shown in Figure 3.3.

Figure 3.3: Maslow's hierarchy of human needs

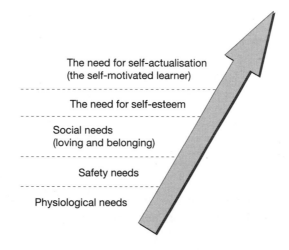

The need for self-actualisation
(the self-motivated learner)

The need for self-esteem

Social needs
(loving and belonging)

Safety needs

Physiological needs

The Unlearned Lesson of Maslow – Summary

Schools often give limited attention to the physiological needs of the students and their learning. For some students the impact of what schools then try to achieve is limited because some of their more basic needs have not been met. Water is not always available, lavatories are often poor, lunches have to be fought for and may be of limited quality. Corridors are crowded, some students feel threatened by the intimidating atmosphere at the change of lessons. Sometimes students are kept outside in the cold at lunchtime. I am not suggesting that the school population is ravaged by thirst and hunger, terrified out of their wits by the prospect of the forthcoming march down the corridor and suffering from lunchtime frostbite. However, I would suggest that some of the population are feeling a milder form of some of these things part of the time, and as a consequence they are not able to respond fully to their learning needs.

- Where do the children in your school spend their lunchtime?
- Where can the children in your school get water when they feel they want some?
- Would you feel comfortable using the children's lavatories?
- If you had to use the corridors in your school eight times a day (in a five-period curriculum), would they add to your stress levels?

If success and the self-esteem that grows from it are seen as a limited commodity, available only to the few, then the whole concept of students as intrinsically motivated learners becomes a shackled wish, inhibited by the failure to provide for the physiological, safety, social and self-esteem needs of all students.

Porter and Lawler

If Maslow was concerned with 'what' motivates people, then his ideas were developed by Porter and Lawler who wanted to understand 'how' people are motivated. Their motivational cycle follows the sequence described in Figure 3.4.

Porter and Lawler believed that the reward that people seek that motivates is both intrinsic and internal. We are intrinsically motivated learners – we want to engage in learning for its own sake, because of how it makes us feel.

The Unlearned Lesson of Porter and Lawler – Summary

How people are motivated to learn becomes accessible by focusing on learning as a process and not the outcomes of learning. The achievement levels will rise, not by demanding that they should but by developing students' meta-abilities, their ability to learn about learning. It is learning where the students will feel the reward that will motivate them, not seeking the rewards that schools spend so much time and effort developing, which miss the targets of motivation and

Figure 3.4: The 'How' of motivation

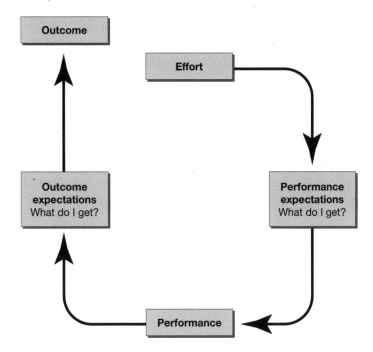

learning. Children may enjoy house points, but do we really believe that they motivate students to learn?

The motivation that Porter and Lawler describe will be engaged by developing the students as meta-learners, young people who understand how they learn and can access the capabilities and emotional states they need to be successful.

Reuven Feuerstein

Reuven Feuerstein introduced the concept of Instrumental Enrichment, having worked with immigrants in Israel at the end of the Second World War. He worked with adolescents, many of whom came from impoverished backgrounds. A large proportion of them appeared to be retarded, though Feuerstein would not accept that the levels of apparent retardation were accurate.

His work brought together both cognitive and emotional thinking and challenged the role of the teacher in the learning process. Feuerstein emphasised that learning is a mediated process. People do not often learn alone; they are usually helped by a teacher, parent or peer. The role of the mediator is to guide the learner to important aspects of the task and ask questions that will stimulate learning. The art of good mediation lies in providing just enough help, providing questions rather than answers and having those questions concerned with 'why' and 'how' rather than 'what'. It is less important for the students to focus on what they have done if they don't have the tools to improve it.

Feuerstein believed that successful learning linked the attitudinal, emotional and belief systems of the student. Mediation was the process through which this would take place. Feuerstein developed a programme that was culture free, and so engaged the student's intrinsic desire to learn. The same effect happens when classrooms are a focus of learning through which the National Curriculum is delivered, rather than a focus of the subject content.

The Unlearned Lesson of Feuerstein – Summary

Feuerstein defined the role of the teacher in learning. He defined the role as mediator; as the conductor of learning through content, not of content as an end in itself. Many good and talented teachers already accept consciously and intuitively the value of Feuerstein's contribution. More can be done to determine how the learning takes place and how questioning can be used to forcefully develop that process.

Carl Rogers

The process of engaging children in their learning through mediation was further developed by Carl Rogers in the 1960s and 70s. Rogers took the view that students know what it is they need to do and that the teacher's role is to bring that understanding to the fore and see it translated into intelligent learning behaviour. The role of the teacher is to bring out what is already there and empower the students to use their own talents to the full.

He was committed to the concept of active listening, of the teacher mediating, learning through awareness of what is being said, and how they judge the student is feeling at the time. The teacher would then feed back to the student and check that what the student had heard and felt was correct. The teacher is creating the basis of emotional literacy, of emotional awareness, enabling and empowering the student to take that forward as emotional learning.

The Unlearned Lessons of Carl Rogers – Summary

Carl Rogers was working in the same domain as Feuerstein and focusing very much on the questions we ask and how they engage children with their learning. He was more focused on emotion than Feuerstein, believing that when students understand the feelings resulting from their behaviour, they will begin to live a more congruent life where behaviour is led by their developing belief system. The lessons for schools are the way in which questions are asked, that they should be focused on how and why, and that both students and teachers should develop their competence as active listeners.

Howard Gardner

Frames of Mind: The Theory of Multiple Intelligences was first published by Howard

Gardner in 1993. He proposes the view that our capacity to be successful in different areas of knowledge, understanding and activity is governed by different areas of the brain. We have the ability to develop our capacity in the following areas:

> Linguistic Intelligence
> Musical Intelligence
> Logical-mathematical Intelligence
> Spatial Intelligence
> Bodily-kinaesthetic Intelligence
> Intra-personal Intelligence
> Interpersonal Intelligence

Multiple intelligence theory is based on the belief that we all have the capability to develop our intelligence in a number of areas. These intelligences build on one another to provide the opportunity for generative learning: the capacity to learn about learning and therefore engage in continual development.

It is the symbolic and metaphoric capability of the brain that creates the bridge between human intelligence and formal learning. It is not a bridge that is crossed in British schools as often as it should be.

Gardner acknowledges the pivotal role of emotion in learning and the power of emotion in the functioning of the mind. The inclusion of interpersonal and intra-personal intelligences makes this very clear.

The Unlearned Lessons of Multiple Intelligences

I suspect that the biggest lesson that has remained unlearnt from Gardner is the realisation that the mind works in a number of different areas of cognition at the same time. The rigid application of key skills in schools, the separation of literacy and numeracy through both phases of the British educational system reflect a limited understanding of the relationship between school learning and the way the mind works.

The importance of emotion and the potency of intrapersonal and interpersonal intelligences remain areas taught as basic skills. It is as valuable as offering a vocational qualification in falling in love.

Bandler and Grinder

The 1970s saw the development of Neuro Linguistic Programming (NLP) under the initial guidance of John Bandler and Richard Grinder. They were concerned with modelling excellence, looking at someone who was successful in a particular area, identifying what they did that made them successful and then teaching those skills to others. This is not to suggest that everyone has the potential to become a scientist like Einstein, an artist like da Vinci or a footballer like George Best. It does mean that everyone can have the tools to become the very best that they can.

This process lead to the development of NLP's 'four pillars' of success. They are:

- Rapport
- Behavioural flexibility
- Sensory acuity
- Outcome orientation

In emotional terms these are concerned with:

- Empathy
- Adaptability
- Awareness
- Ambition/motivation

The NLP movement has been developing and growing since the initial work by Bandler and Grinder, and has developed some practical and powerful exercises and skills in learning and personal development. These skills would include learning:

- The physiology of rapport – modelling.
- The language of rapport – understanding how the language we use is a window to our learning style and how by being aware of the learning style of others we can greatly increase the power of our own communication.
- The ability to engage people whom we may find difficult.
- Realising what we want and how we can achieve our goals.

Unlearned Lessons of NLP – Summary

NLP offers skills and practical strategies that can help to develop our abilities in the four pillars of NLP as well as offering ways of working that will help people who have limiting and negative beliefs. It also provides the opportunity to examine learning strategies in close detail and learn from the success of others. NLP provides a rich insight into learning and can bring about some amazing results with individuals and groups.

Affective Education and Emotional Intelligence

Emotional intelligence has its history in the affective education movement. Many of the lessons in learning that have been available were not taken, though they have the power and potency to make a contribution to the development of an emotionally intelligent school where learning and achievement are available to all.

Chapter Four

Self Review – The Habits, Attitudes, Beliefs and Emotions of Success

"Winning is a habit. Unfortunately so is losing"
Vince Lombardi
American football coach

Attitudes, habits and beliefs become the observable outcomes of emotional intelligence. They become the point at which students experience the benefits of an emotional intelligence programme, and the point at which you, as the teacher, can begin to experience the progress that is being made.

Assessment of emotional intelligence is concerned with developing your self-awareness and self-review skills so that each individual student can determine the progress they are making. Self-review is part of the process of students taking responsibility for their own learning. Traditional assessment is predominantly what one person does to another, and there is little evidence that it has any positive effect on performance. Self-review is the student monitoring their own progress towards a valued goal.

Self-review does not dis-empower the teacher as they are still monitoring and assessing the outcomes of education and playing a powerful role in mediating the students' learning. The teacher will also be able to judge whether any learning programme is having an effect on these crucial measures of educational outcome, the KS3, GCSE and A-level results.

What follows are examples of how you can help students to develop their own strategies of self-awareness and self-review. I have picked different approaches for each of the 'emotions of success' so that you will have a feel for the variety of approaches that can be taken.

The programme of review will follow this process:

- Classroom outcomes of the Magic Learning Programme.
- What are the 'emotions of success'?
- How can I help the student develop self-review procedures in these areas?
  1. Ambition and motivation – Where do I want to get to?
  2. Optimism – Have I the resilience to achieve my goals?
  3. Empathy – Can I engage the support of those who will help my learning, and to whom I may offer my expertise?

4. Integrity – Am I learning those things that are congruent with my personal beliefs and values?
5. Self-awareness – The quality through which this will be achieved.

- Habits, attitudes and beliefs of achievement.
- Collaborative assessment in the classroom.

One of the exciting things about reviewing the students' development during the Magic Learning Programme is the ease with which they begin to realise that they are fabulous learners and the experience you will have of that progress. You will see them become 'magicians of learning'.

Classroom Outcomes of Emotional Learning

What you will see, hear and feel in your classroom:

- Emotional self-awareness
  - Improvement in the students recognising and naming emotions
  - They are better able to understand the causes of their feelings
  - Recognising the difference between feelings and actions
- Managing emotions
  - Better frustration tolerance and anger management
  - Fewer verbal put-downs, fights and classroom disruptions
  - Better able to express anger appropriately without fighting
  - Fewer suspensions and expulsions
  - Less aggressive or self-destructive behaviour
  - More positive feelings about self, school and family
  - Better at handling stress
  - Less loneliness and social anxiety
- Harnessing emotions productively
  - More responsibility
  - Better able to focus on the task at hand and pay attention
  - Less impulsive and more self-controlled
  - Improved scores on achievement tests
- Empathy reading emotions
  - Better able to take another person's perspective
  - Improved empathy and sensitivity to another's feelings
  - Better at listening to others
  - Better able to see the value of others as a learning resource
- Handling relationships
  - Increased ability to understand and analyse relationships
  - Better at resolving conflicts and negotiating outcomes
  - Better at resolving problems in relationships
  - More assertive and skilled in communicating
  - More popular and outgoing
  - More concerned and considerate
  - More democratic in dealing with others
  - More social and harmonious in groups

Emotions for Success

What are the emotions that will deliver these outcomes? Getting this right is crucial to the programme and understanding where and how the development of the students will be taking place.

What are the specific emotions that will give the students success in the classroom and in their life? I took five models of emotional learning and compared them in order to see if there were common threads running through; to see if they would offer an insight into what might be seen as a core of emotions where emotional literacy can be focused. The five models I took are:

- Daniel Goleman, *Emotional Intelligence*
- Cooper and Sawaf, *Executive EQ – Emotional Intelligence in business*
- The Emotional Intelligence Institute of Sweden
- Higgs and Dulewicz, *Making sense of Emotional Intelligence*
- Michael Bernard, *You can do it Education*

I developed a common language describing the emotions used in each of the five models. The aim was to try to avoid a semantic argument, which would be distracting and unnecessary. You may wish to create your own list and your own view of what constitutes success emotions. The important issue is to engage the process of deciding which emotions you believe will create emotional learning and not argue over semantic nuances. Test your hypothesis: if you are right, operate it; if it can be improved, change it. The same must apply to the students if the course is to reflect the values and principles of EQ. They must work out which emotions will bring them success, take responsibility for their decisions, test their belief and amend it in order to maximise their success. The following work should not be seen as a tablet of stone, rather a starting place. The EQ work I researched can be summarised as follows:

Cooper and Sawaf

Emotions of success
- Emotional literacy
  1. Emotional honesty
  2. Emotional energy
  3. Emotional feedback
  4. Emotional connection

- Emotional fitness
  1. Resilience
  2. Constructive discontent
  3. Trust
  4. Authentic presence

> **Emotional learning**
> Self-awareness
> Motivation
> Self-confidence
> Intuition
> Self-esteem
> Creativity
> Trust
> Integrity

- Emotional depth
  1. Influence
  2. Integrity
  3. Commitment
  4. Potential

- Emotional alchemy
  1. Intuitive flow
  2. Reflection
  3. Creating the future

> **Emotional learning**
> Self-esteem
> Creativity
> Trust
> Integrity
> Congruence
> Integrity
> Commitment
> Ambition
> Relaxed focus
> Empathy
> Goal orientation

Emotional Intelligence Institute of Sweden

Emotions of success
- Self-knowledge
- Empathy
- Responsibility
- Communication
- Conflict resolution

> **Emotional learning**
> Self-awareness
> Empathy
> Adaptability
> Optimism
> Self-esteem

From responsibility to adaptability may be a jump that needs explanation. I believe that responsibility is probably the single most misunderstood concept today. I simply and literally understand it to mean 'the ability to respond'. To be responsible successfully requires many talents, including integrity, empathy, self-esteem, optimism and a sense of purpose. If responsibility is to have values at its core then, crucially, it has to reflect the ability to adapt.

Higgs and Dulewicz

Emotions of success
- Perceptive listening
- Sensitivity
- Flexibility
- Achievement orientation
- Energy
- Stress tolerance
- Resilience
- Influence
- Negotiating ability
- Decisiveness
- Ascendancy
- Impact
- Integrity
- Motivating others
- Leadership

> **Emotional learning**
> Empathy
> Awareness
> Adaptability
> Ambition
> Motivation
> Self-esteem
> Integrity
> Optimism
> Confidence
> Goal orientation
> Risk taking

Daniel Goleman

Emotions of success
- Self-awareness
- Empathy
- Reflection
- Self Regulation
- Motivation
- Social skills
- Creativity

Emotional learning
Self-awareness
Empathy
Reflection
Adaptability
Motivation
Empathy
Creativity

Michael Bernard

Emotions of success
- Confidence
- Organisation
- Persistence
- Getting along

Emotional learning
Self-esteem
Goal orientation
Optimism
Empathy

What starts to emerge are some core emotions that when managed can be used to powerfully enhance the chances of success both in the classroom and in life. They are not intended as a definitive list. I don't believe any such list exists. It would represent a paradox within emotional intelligence for anyone to try to pretend otherwise. What does exist is a list of emotions that will certainly have a positive impact when they are there and a very negative impact in their absence. I would include in my list:

- Self-awareness
- Ambition
- Integrity
- Motivation
- Optimism
- Self-esteem
- Creativity
- Empathy

This is still too long and complex to work within a school. If, however, I ask the fundamental questions that a student needs to be able to answer about their learning, then I am able to create a comprehensive and manageable view of emotional success. The questions I would ask are:

1. What do you want to learn?
2. Do you believe you can?
3. How can others help you?
4. Is this learning congruent with your values and beliefs?
5. What sort of learner are you?

The purpose of learning is to identify and fulfil potential and so the following emotional states would be essential if the student is to successfully answer the questions about their learning:

- Question 1 – **Ambition/motivation**
- Question 2 – **Optimism**
- Question 3 – **Empathy**
- Question 4 – **Integrity**
- Question 5 – **Self-awareness**

How then can students review their current state, and where they want to be in their expert use of these emotions to further their learning?

Ambition/Motivation

Do you have goals in your life towards which you aspire? If you don't know where you are going, you will never know when you have got there and rarely feel the pleasure of success.

Setting personal goals in school and in life is crucial to success. Those goals must reflect your own sense of ambition, be motivating to you and congruent with your sense of personal integrity. How successful you are at this moment can be understood by using the exercises that follow.

Activity: Wheel of identity
We are all a number of different people, at different times and in different places. You may be a student, a sports person, a musician, a brother, a friend and so on.

Fill in the 'who I am wheel' shown in Figure 4.1, adding as many extra spokes as you can. You might think of sister, brother, guitar player, friend and so on.

When you have done that, ask yourself what goals you have for each of those pieces of you. Mark on the spoke where you currently are in relation to those goals.

Having goals does not mean they are appropriate or the right size. Deciding that your goal is to be happy may be too big and not specific enough to be achieved easily by conscious effort. Deciding that your goal is to get fit may not be big enough to motivate. When you are fit, what will that give you? This may start to make your goals the right size.

Activity: Setting goals the right size
Look at the metaphor you drew of your life. Remember how you want it to look, sound and feel.

Figure 4.1: Wheel of identity

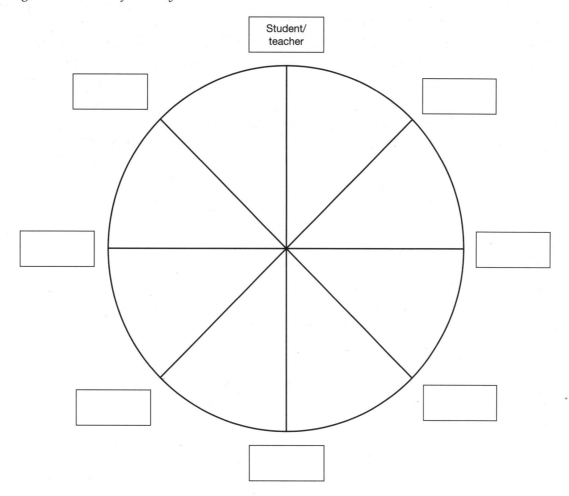

You should now take each of the spokes of your wheel and set goals for each one. You can write these up in your Learning Journal next to your wheel.

Your goals should be SMART:

S – specific: *They should not be too big, though they should make a difference.*
M – measurable: *How will you know when you have achieved your goal?*
A – attainable: *Make sure your goal is something you can achieve.*
R – resource: *What do you need to achieve your goal?*
T – Timed: *When will you have achieved your goal?*

Thinking about these things, write down what your goal will be for each of your spokes. You should do this in your Learning Journal.

To prepare each one, follow the goal-setting sheet shown in Figure 4.2.

Figure 4.2: The goal-setting sheet

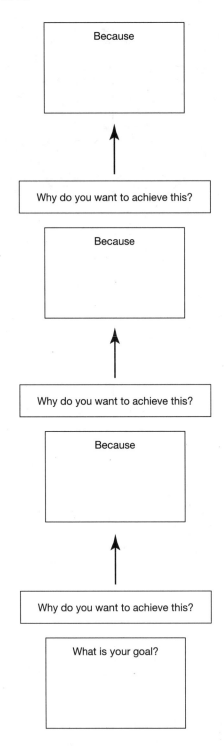

If you find that this is not working, it may be that your goal is too big and needs to be broken down in order that you can understand what needs to be done. Try this following exercise.

Ask yourself, 'What is my goal?' and write your answer in the box in Figure 4.3.

Figure 4.3: Goals

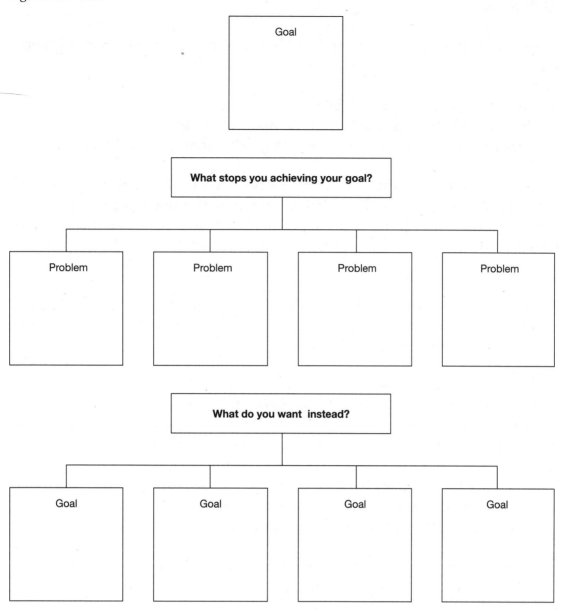

To make sure your goals will motivate you, test them against the mnemonic PACES:

P – Are they **Positive?**
A – Will they lead to **Achievement?**
C – Are they within your **Control?**
E – What **Effect** will they have?
S – Will they help you to **Step into the future?**

The goal-setting exercises will help the students develop their own sense of direction, their own goals, which they can test and, if they are working, implement.

Optimism

The second emotion of success is optimism, which is concerned with the belief that:

1. Something may not last for ever.
2. It may not have an impact on every aspect of my life.
3. I may not be to blame. Neither may any other individual or group.

Optimism is crucial to our success as learners, to our ability to see comments made to us as feedback and something we can learn from and control. It is the very bedrock of seeing feedback and not failure, of realising that we all fall down at times, though this is less important than the belief in our ability to pick ourselves up.

Your levels of optimism can be identified by using the questionnaires designed by Martin Seligman in his book *Learned Optimism*. There are two recorded below, one for adults and one for students.

Activity 6: How optimistic am I? – optimism for adults
Although you may not agree with the way all the responses sound, don't try to think what you *should* say but what you are more *likely* to say.

1. The project you are in charge of is a great success (F)
    a. You watch closely what everyone else is doing 1
    b. Everyone tried really hard 0

2. You have an argument with a friend and then you make up (B)
    a. I forgive him/her...0
    b. I am usually forgiving 1

3. You get lost driving to a friend's house (E)
    a. I missed a turn 1
    b. My friend gave me wrong directions...0

4. Your spouse/boyfriend/girlfriend gives you a surprise present (A)
    a. He/she got a pay rise 0
    b. I took them out to dinner the night before....................................1

5. You forget a friend's birthday (D)
    a. I am not very good at remembering birthdays...............................1
    b. I was busy with other things 0

6. You get a flower from a secret admirer (D)
    a. I am attractive to him/her 0
    b. I am a popular person...1

7. You are elected to a community office (D)
    a. I put a lot of time into trying to get the post..............................0
    b. I just work very hard at everything I do.................................1

8. You miss an important meeting (C)
    a. Sometimes I just forget things 1
    b. I sometimes forget to check what I should be doing...................0

9. You are not elected to a community office (E)
    a. I didn't put enough time into getting the post 1
    b. The person who won knew more people 0

10. You host a successful dinner (B)
    a. I was particularly charming that night 0
    b. I am very good at holding parties 1

11. You stop a crime by calling the police (F)
    a. A strange noise caught my attention..1
    b. I was very alert that day..0

12. You were extremely healthy all year (F)
    a. Not many other people were ill so I didn't catch anything..........0
    b. I made sure I ate a healthy diet and had some good exercise......1

13. The library sends you a reminder that a book is overdue (A)
    a. When I really get involved in reading a book I sometimes
        forget when it is due 1
    b. I was so involved in doing other things that I forgot
        to return the book..0

14. Your shares make a lot of money (B)
    a. My broker took on something new 1
    b. My broker is a great investor...0

15. You win a competition (B)
    a. I was feeling unbeatable...0
    b. I train hard..1

16. You fail an important exam (C)
    a. I was not as clever as the other people taking the test.................0
    b. I didn't prepare as well as I should have 1

17. You prepare a special meal for a friend and they barely touch
    the food (C)
    a. I wasn't a good cook 0
    b. I did it too quickly..1

18. You lose a competition that you have been practising for a long time (C)
    a. I am not very good at competitions...1
    b. I am not very good at that particular skill.................................0

19. Your car runs out of petrol on a dark street late at night (E)
    a. I didn't make check to see how much petrol I had......................1
    b. The petrol gauge was broken 0

20. You lose your temper with a friend (A)
    a. He/she is always nagging me...0
    b. He/she is always looking for a fight..1

21. You are fined for not returning your tax form on time (A)
    a. I always put off doing my tax return 1
    b. I was just lazy about getting my tax return done this year 0

22. You ask a person out for a date and they say no (C)
    a. I was a wreck that day..1
    b. I got tongue-tied when I asked them 0

23. A game show host picks you to take part in the show (F)
    a. I was sitting in the right seat 0
    b. I looked the most enthusiastic..1

24. People kept asking me to dance at a party (B)
    a. I am outgoing at parties 0
    b. I really was good fun that night...1

25. You buy a friend a present, and they don't like it (E)
    a. I don't put enough thought into buying presents........................0
    b. He/she has very picky tastes 1

26. You do exceptionally well at a job interview (B)
    a. I felt very confident during the interview 0
    b. I interview very well...1

27. You tell a joke and everyone laughs (F)
    a. The joke was funny 0
    b. My timing was perfect..1

28. Your boss gives you too little time to finish a project, but you finish it anyway (D)
    a. I am a clever student...1
    b. I am efficient...0

29. You are feeling run down lately (A)
    a. I never get a chance to relax 0
    b. I have been really busy this week..1

30. You ask someone to dance and they say no (E)
    a. I am not a very good dancer..1
    b. He/she doesn't like to dance..0

31. You save someone from choking to death (D)
    a. You know life-saving skills 1
    b. You know what to do in a crisis..0

32. Your romantic partner wants to cool things off for a while (C)
    a. I am too self-centred..0
    b. I didn't spend enough time with him/her 1

33. A friend says something that hurts your feelings (A)
    a. He/she always blurts things out without thinking of others 1
    b. My friend was in a bad mood and took it out on me...................0

34. Your employer comes to you for advice (D)
    a. I am an expert in the area they asked about 0
    b. I am good at giving useful advice 1

35. A friend thanks you for helping them get through a bad time (D)
    a. I enjoyed helping them through a tough time..1
    b. I care about people 0

36. You had a great time at a party (F)
    a. Everyone was friendly..1
    b. I was friendly 0

37. Your doctor tells you that you are very fit (D)
    a. I take a lot of exercise..1
    b. I am very health conscious..0

38. Your romantic partner takes you away for a romantic weekend (B)
    a. He/she needs to get away for a few days..0
    b. He/she likes to explore new areas..1

39. Your doctor tells you that you eat too much sugar (E)
    a. I don't pay much attention to what I eat..1
    b. You can't avoid sugar, it's in everything 0

40. You are asked to be the leader of an important project (B)
    a. I was asked to lead the last project and that was a success..........0
    b. I am a good leader..1

41. You and your partner have been fighting a great deal (E)
    a. I have been feeling a bit cranky lately.................................1
    b. He/she has been aggressive lately 0

42. You keep falling down a lot when skiing (A)
    a. It is very difficult to do...1
    b. The slopes were very icy 0

43. You win a prestigious award (D)
    a. I solved an important problem..0
    b. I was the best person..1

44. Your shares are at an all-time low (C)
    a. I didn't know much about the business climate at the time 1
    b. I made a poor choice of stocks 0

45. You win the lottery (F)
    a. It was pure chance...0
    b. I picked the right numbers..1

46. You gain weight over the holidays and can't lose it (A)
    a. Diets don't work in the long run 1
    b. The diet I tried didn't work 0

47. You are in hospital and not many people come to visit (E)
    a. I am irritable when I am sick..1
    b. My friends aren't very good at visiting in hospital 0

48. They won't honour your credit card at the shop (C)
    a. I sometimes overestimate how much money I have.....................1
    b. I sometimes forget to pay my credit card bill 0

Marking your questionnaire
Add up your scores for each letter

A......   D......

B......   E......

C......   F......

Your **A** scores cover the area **'permanently bad'**.
Your **B** score covers the area **'permanently good'**.
Your **C** score covers the area **'pervasively bad'**.
Your **D** score covers the area **'pervasively good'**.
Your **E** score covers the area **'personalised bad'**.
Your **F** score covers the area **'personalised good'**.

To each of these individual areas you can apply the following:

0–1	You are very optimistic in this area
2–3	You are moderately optimistic
4	Average
5–6	Quite pessimistic
7–8	Very pessimistic

1. Add up (pessimism)   A + C + E = _____
2. Add up (optimism)   B + D + F = _____

Overall score
Pessimism

3–6	Very optimistic
6–9	Moderately optimistic
10–11	Average
12–14	Moderately pessimistic
14 and above	Very pessimistic

Optimism

19 or above	Very optimistic
17–19	Moderately optimistic
14–16	Average
11–13	Quite pessimistic
10 or less	Very pessimistic

O – P scores = ...

Above 8	Very optimistic
6–8	Moderately optimistic
3–5	Average
1–2	Moderately pessimistic
0 or below	Very pessimistic

Adapted from the work of Martin Seligman – *Learned Optimism*

Activity 6: Children's attributional style questionnaire

1. You get an A on a test (D)
    a. I am smart...0
    b. I am good at the subject that the test was in. 1

2. You play a game with some friends and you win (E)
    a. The people I played with did not play the game well.........................0
    b. I play that game well 1

3. You spend the night at a friend's house and you have a good time (D)
    a. My friend was in a friendly mood that night.................................0
    b. Everyone in my friend's family was in a friendly mood that night ..1

4. You go on a holiday with a group of people and you have fun (E)
    a. I was in a good mood...1
    b. The people I was with were in a good mood 0

5. All of your friends catch a cold except you (B)
    a. I have been healthy lately 1
    b. I am a healthy person 0

6. Your pet gets run over by a car (F)
    a. I don't take good care of my pets 1
    b. Drivers are not cautious enough 0

7. Some kids you know say that they don't like you (F)
    a. Once in a while people are mean to me 0
    b. Once in a while I am mean to other people...............................1

8. You get very good grades (E)
    a. School work is simple...0
    b. I am a hard worker 1

9. You meet a friend and your friend tells you that you look nice (B)
    a. My friend felt like praising the way people looked that day 1
    b. Usually my friend praises the way people look 0

10. A good friend tells you that they hate you (F)
    a. My friend was in a bad mood that day.....................................1
    b. I wasn't nice to my friend that day 0

11. You tell a joke and no one laughs (F)
    a. I don't tell jokes well...1
    b. The joke is so well known that it is no longer funny 0

12. Your teacher gives a lesson and no one understands it (C)
    a. I didn't pay attention to anything that day 0
    b. I didn't pay attention when my teacher was talking 1

13. You fail a test (A)
    a. My teacher makes hard tests..0
    b. The past few weeks my teacher has made hard tests 1

14. You gain a lot of weight and start to look fat (F)
    a. The food I have to eat is fattening..0
    b. I like fattening foods...1

15. A person steals money from you (C)
    a. That person is dishonest 1
    b. People are dishonest 0

16. Your parents praise something you make (E)
    a. I am good at making some things 1
    b. My parents like some things I make 0

17. You play a game and you win some money (D)
    a. I am a lucky person...0
    b. I am lucky when I play games 1

18. You almost drown when swimming in a river (A)
    a. I am not a very cautious person 0
    b. Some days I am not a cautious person 1

19. You are invited to a lot of parties (E)
    a. A lot of people have been acting friendly toward me lately 1
    b. I have been acting friendly towards a lot of people lately 0

20. A grown-up yells at you (C)
    a. That person yelled at the first person they saw 0
    b. That person yelled at a lot of people they saw that day.....................1

21. You do a project with a group of kids and it turns out badly (C)
    a. I don't work well with the people in the group.....................0
    b. I never work well with a group 1

22. You make a new friend (E)
    a. I am a nice person 0
    b. The people that I meet are nice..1

23. You have been getting along well with your family (B)
    a. I am easy to get along with when I am with my family.....................1
    b. Once in a while I am easy to get along with when I am with my family 0

24. You try to sell some sweets but no one will buy any (A)
    a. Lately a lot of children have been selling things so no one wants
       to buy things from children..0
    b. People don't like to buy things from children.....................1

25. You play a game and you win (D)
    a. Sometimes I try as hard as I can at games 0
    b. Sometimes I try as hard as I can 1

26. You get a bad mark at school (F)
    a. I am stupid 1
    b. Teachers are unfair markers 0

27. You walk into a door and bang your nose (C)
    a. I wasn't looking where I was going..1
    b. I have been careless lately...0

28. You miss the ball and your team loses the game (A)
    a. I didn't try hard when I was playing that day.......................1
    b. I don't usually try hard when I am playing games...............0

29. You twist your ankle during a PE lesson (F)
    a. We have been playing dangerous sports during the past
       few weeks at school..0
    b. I have been clumsy in my PE lessons lately 1

30. Your parents take you to the beach and you have a good time (D)
    a. Everything at the beach was nice that day 0
    b. The weather at the beach was nice that day.........................1

31. You catch a train that is so late that you miss the film (A)
    a. The past few days there have been problems with the trains
       being on time 0
    b. The trains are almost never on time......................................1

32. Your mother makes your favourite dinner for you (D)
    a. There are a few things that my mother does to please me...............1
    b. My mother likes to please me 0

33. A team that you are on loses a game (A)
    a. The team members do not play well together......................1
    b. That day the team members did not play well together 0

34. You finish your homework quickly (D)
    a. Lately I have been doing everything quickly 0
    b. Lately I have been doing school work quickly......................1

35. Your teacher asks you a question and you give the wrong answer (A)
    a. I get nervous when I have to answer questions....................0
    b. That day I got nervous when I had to answer questions 1

36. You get on the wrong bus and get lost (A)
    a. That day I wasn't paying attention to what was going on..............1
    b. I usually don't pay attention to what is going on................0

37. You go to a theme park and have a good time (D)
    a. I usually enjoy myself at theme parks 1
    b. I usually enjoy myself...0

38. An older student slaps you in the face (F)
    a. I teased their younger brother...0
    b. Their younger brother said I had teased him........................1

39. You get all the presents you want on your birthday (B)
    a. People always guess what presents I want for my birthday..............1
    b. This birthday people guessed which presents I wanted.................0

40. You go on holiday in the country and have a wonderful time (B)
    a. The country is a beautiful place to be.............................1
    b. The time of the year that we went was beautiful...................0

41. Your neighbours ask you over for dinner (B)
    a. Sometimes people are in kind moods.............................1
    b. People are kind...0

42. You have a supply teacher and they like you (B)
    a. I was well behaved during class that day........................0
    b. I am almost always well behaved during class....................1

43. You make your friends happy (B)
    a. I am a fun person to be with....................................1
    b. Sometimes I am a fun person to be with.........................0

44. You get a free ice-cream cone (E)
    a. I was friendly to the ice-cream man that day....................1
    b. The ice-cream man was feeling friendly that day.................0

45. At your friend's party the magician asks you to help (E)
    a. It was just luck that I got picked..............................0
    b. I looked really interested in what was going on.................1

46. You try to persuade a friend to go to the cinema with you
    though they won't (C)
    a. That day they did not feel like doing anything..................1
    b. That day they did not feel like going to the cinema.............0

47. Your parents get divorced (C)
    a. It is hard for people to get along when they are married........1
    b. It is hard for my parents to get along when they are married....0

48. You have been trying to get into a club and you don't get in (C)
    a. I don't get along well with other people........................1
    b. I don't get along well with the people in the club..............0

Adapted from the work of Martin Seligman – *Learned Optimism*

Marking your questionnaire
Before the students mark their questionnaire they must complete the following exercise.
It may be advisable for them to do it before they complete the questionnaire.

Activity Sheet: Metaphors R us

Metaphors are great ways of being able to describe how we feel to ourselves and to others. They are ways in which you take one thing to describe something else. For example, I might use the following metaphors:

> When I feel happy I feel like a sunny day.
> When I feel happy I feel like a beach.
> When I feel sad I feel like a punctured football.
> When I feel confident I feel like great white horse.

Think of a theme for your metaphors. It could be:

> *The weather, animals, places, sport, clothes or anything else you can think of.*

The most important thing is that the metaphor means something to you.

Think about each of the situations below and write your own metaphor for them.

1. I feel happy
2. I feel gloomy
3. I feel confident
4. I feel anxious
5. I feel it was my fault
6. I feel successful

Add up your scores for each letter:

A......   D......

B......   E......

C......   F......

Now you need to do some maths.

1. **A + C + E =**

2. **B + D + F =**

3. **Answer to 2. – Answer to 1. =**

Now look at your metaphors in the 'metaphors R us' exercise.

If you have a score of 6 or more, you often feel like your metaphors for 1, 3 and 6.
If you have a score of 3–5 then you sometimes feel like the metaphors 1, 3 and 6.
If you have a score of 1–2 then you sometimes feel like the metaphors 2, 4 and 5.
If you have a score of 0 or below then you often feel like the metaphors 2, 4 and 5.

This exercise is then followed up in the Magic Learning Programme to show the students that however they feel at the moment does not mean that they have to carry on like it, unless they choose to.

Empathy

Developing processes of self-review with empathy can be approached in a number of ways. What I shall describe is chosen to illustrate the variey of ways you can help your students to become natural reviewers of their own learning.

Empathy is the ability to be aware of the feelings and motives of others and learn to use them to your mutual benefit as learners. Being successfully empathetic is built on an optimism and trust of others. Trust that every action has a positive intent, then you will be able to use the resources the other person has to help your learning. If you do not trust the integrity of the other person's actions then anger will cloud your vision and judgement and your very intolerance will inhibit your learning.

My son may be told to go and tidy his room. He may go to his room and 20 minutes later still be playing on his Gameboy. His room still resembles the outcome of a particularly violent battle. His positive intent is that he wants to enjoy his Gameboy. His learning need is to be aware of other priorities at times and learn to delay his personal pleasure. Anger may be appropriate, though I can use it successfully when I have understood his motives; the positive intention behind his action. If I believe he is just a disobedient little boy then my anger will be different and probably less successful as his learning will be very different.

One way of developing self-review of empathy can be done through the students' Learning Journal.

The students can record the answers to the following questions and then you can provide the opportunity for them to share their answers with other students.

1. Think of something that someone did or said that really bothered or upset you.
2. What was this person trying to achieve for themselves?
3. How did what they did or said stop you getting what you wanted?
4. What could you have said or done to still achieve your goal in this circumstance?

5. How did you feel when you let this person decide what you should have or do?
6. How did you need to feel to get what you wanted from this situation?

Put up your video screen and remember what happened, see what you saw, hear what you heard and feel what you felt.

Now remember a time when you felt those emotions that you need to succeed.

Go into your film and take those emotions to the you in the film.

Now rerun the film, feeling what you need to feel, and see, hear and feel the success.

There are a great number of ways of beginning a programme of continual self-review and development. They will all appeal to some students, reflecting their learning and thinking styles. Give them choices from which they can develop their own strategies.

Integrity and Self-awareness

The very essence of the Magic Learning Programme is to empower students, to enable them to be aware of their emotions and how they can use them to support their learning in every decision or action they take. To achieve this, there needs to be an increasing sense of whether what they are doing is congruent with who they are. The developing sense of belief and identity within the levels of learning will ensure that the students develop their own sense of integrity, their own belief in right and wrong.

One thing that can be achieved during this period of growth is to help the students develop their skills of engaging in the personal dialogue that leads to congruent decisions being taken. Part of that is done through the questions we ask students. Concentrating on 'how' and 'why' is a very straightforward, yet potent, tool. Teaching the students the physiology of personal reflection will also help you to mediate in their learning and for them to have the skills to succeed. Looking down and to the left is usually the best way of engaging in personal dialogue. For left-handed people it may be looking down and to the right. Giving students the opportunity to reflect on moral issues and making them aware of the way that physiology can help will allow them to develop their own skills.

Habits, Attitudes and Beliefs

The Magic Learning Programme will develop the emotional literacy and emotional learning of the student. As a result of the programme, the observable behaviours of emotion will change. Our habits, attitudes and beliefs are all self-taught. We were not born with them, we learned them. Emotional learning will allow students to reconsider what they have learnt, keep those things that are positive and change those that are inhibiting learning.

Figure 4.4: Habits, attitudes and beliefs

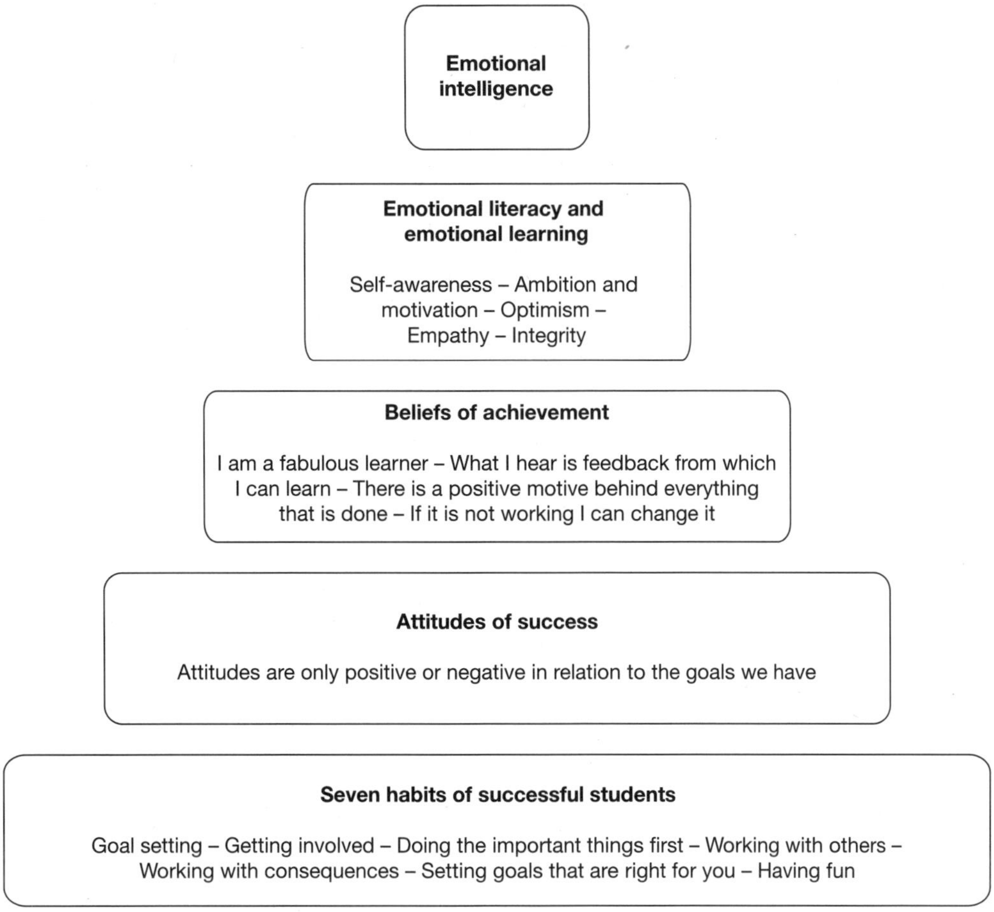

Emotional intelligence

Emotional literacy and emotional learning

Self-awareness – Ambition and motivation – Optimism – Empathy – Integrity

Beliefs of achievement

I am a fabulous learner – What I hear is feedback from which I can learn – There is a positive motive behind everything that is done – If it is not working I can change it

Attitudes of success

Attitudes are only positive or negative in relation to the goals we have

Seven habits of successful students

Goal setting – Getting involved – Doing the important things first – Working with others – Working with consequences – Setting goals that are right for you – Having fun

Chapter Five

Emotional Intelligence and Social Inclusion – A Case Study

Emotional Intelligence is a powerful process of raising achievement for all children throughout the age and ability range. I have chosen to describe this particular case study as it concerns the most difficult children to reach and paints a vivid picture of the impact of an EQ project.

I was approached by an 11–16 school which by most measures is extremely successful. They were finding difficulty engaging a group of disaffected year 10 (15-year-old) students. The school had tried to support the students' learning by extending the time they spent at the local technical college. The students were already successfully following a vocational course at the college and the school decided to build on this and have the students follow their Spanish course there as well. Unfortunately, twelve of the students grasped the opportunity to be away from school with such enthusiasm that the college said they were no longer prepared to take them.

The behaviour of the students at the college had been so disruptive that there was a real probability that the students would be excluded from school. The Head of Modern Languages and a Learning Assistant who had worked with these young people for two years were determined that something positive should be done. They persuaded the Senior Management Team of the school to invest in a six-week experiment in Emotional Intelligence and I was asked to design and run the programme.

The background of the students was far from unusual and would be mirrored in many schools nationally. At home there was evidence of emotional as well as physical abuse and at school they had had a great deal of experience of school sanctions. Outwardly the students didn't care and their behaviour appeared to be designed to make sure they got into as much trouble as possible.

The school was working hard to do all it could for these students. There were dedicated and committed staff but the problem seemed to be that the learning environment was often built on compliance rather than commitment to learning. As soon as the students were away from effective control they would do all they could to disturb the learning of others.

The Beginning

The initial project lasted for six weeks and was designed to allow the students to reframe their experience of learning, to empower them to take a positive perspective and to realise that learning in school can have a positive impact on their success in the classroom and in their lives.

My first meeting with the students began with two of them bundling into the classroom and a third coming in and lying on the floor. Other students came and went for the first 10 minutes, making it very clear who they (rightly) believed had the power and that they were going to exercise it.

The session continued with intermittent engagement by the students and a lot of posturing. It ended with the students feeling confused and resentful. They were now being denied the opportunity to go to the college and had lost the freedom associated with that. This was powerfully represented by them now having to wear school uniform, which they hadn't had to do at the college. The students had no real idea of who I was, what the course was for and why they were being 'punished' in this way. It was an interesting start.

The planning of the programme was a realistic appraisal of the possible. Emotional Intelligence is the application of knowledge and understanding which can have a powerful impact within the environment of schools. In the planning I used the 'levels of learning' as a template in order to make sure that the programme had the maximum impact on the students' learning. The levels of learning are:

> Identity – Who? of learning
> Belief – Why? of learning
> Capability – How? of learning
> Behaviour – What? of learning
> Environment – When? and Where? of learning

Environment

It was crucial that the students had an environment in which they could learn and in which they could begin to develop trust.

The classroom we had was far from helpful. It was no one's fault, merely being the room that was available. It did reflect the difficulties schools often have in creating learning environments. Given the acute nature of the project, the diffi-culties with the room represented a real challenge. It was a thoroughfare between lessons and, with another year 10 class next door, the group's peers would come through after the first hour. The level of disruption and the oppor-tunities this offered the students were predictable. It was also a room that gave access to one of the departmental videos and so we found ourselves being asked to decamp at a moment's notice as others wanted to use the facilities.

The ideal environment could not be created. It was crucial that enough change took place to make the learning of the programme possible. We took steps to physically change the environment. The students were stopped from using it as a thoroughfare between lessons and the students on the course were told that they did not have to wear school uniform. This also helped the work that was done to change the students' perception of their environment. The room was described to the students as a 'bubble' that rested outside of the usual relationships and expectations of school. However, if the students went beyond the expectations and culture of the 'bubble', they would effectively be back in school and subject to school expectations and sanctions. This metaphor worked well and enabled the students to re-conceptualise and reframe their environment.

Behaviour

The students drew up a code of conduct for the programme, which included some great discussion about what they should do if they felt that they could not cope at any time during the two hours. These were young people who might have spent the night before on the street, who might have been taking drugs of some form very recently, or who had had a very negative time within school that day. They came up with the idea of a quiet area, where they could go, have their own space and that this would be fine.

Capability

The first part of the programme was to open up the 'channels of learning'. The experiences the students had had, both in school and in their lives, meant that they were emotionally blocked off from the process of positive learning. They had learnt some very powerful strategies to protect themselves from being put down emotionally and in some cases physically. Learning that they could understand what was happening to them in a different way, and develop new skills that they could apply, was the first step that had to be taken. This is sometimes called 'reframing' the experience.

A process was introduced at the beginning of each lesson called 'debunking'. Here the students could talk about anything that had happened to them that was currently 'running a tape' in the back of their mind; things that they were literally talking to themselves about. To begin to talk about these issues is the first stage in dealing with them and starts to create the openness for learning. The first two sessions were characterised by a lot of fantasy, things that they professed to have done which were just designed to shock. As they got no response they gradually started to do what they needed to do, which was to talk about what they were thinking. Once a concern has been articulated, then your mind is on a journey to resolve the problem as you see it. The sessions were an opportunity for the staff to guide the students to understand their experience and to reframe it in a more positive way. The positivity comes from feeling empowered in the way you respond, rather than in trying to believe that a very negative experience was really good fun. The staff worked to make sure that the integrity of the learning remained with the students. No advice was given, even though it was often sought. Advice and responsibility are powerful issues in the whole programme of empowerment.

The programme began to have an effect and there was a gradual change in the behaviour of the students. This was no 'Road to Damascus' story , though it was a story of a group of young people slowly starting to take more responsibility for their lives and realising that their actions had consequences, which could be positive for them.

Belief

"Whether we believe we can or whether we believe we can't we will probably be right", said Henry Ford. Our behaviour follows our belief, and the sustainable success of the project would come about when the students had a different set of beliefs about themselves, their capability and their power to have a positive influence on their world. Belief change can be brought about with remarkable ease. The simplicity of the process is dependent on motivation. The students at the start did not believe there was any other way of seeing, and consequently behaving, towards their world other than the way they did. The key to them starting to reframe their view of the world, change their beliefs, emotional state and capacity to learn, was through developing capability. If we believe we can achieve little, then we aspire to little and prove ourselves right. If we believe we can achieve a great deal, then we aspire to that level and again prove ourselves right. That is not to say that there aren't difficulties along the way, though it is the context within which we see those events that determines how we respond to them and then go forward.

As the programme progressed, the rising levels of capability and competence were having an effect on the students' self-esteem, aspiration and achievement and we began to get feedback from other staff describing the positive changes they were seeing and hearing in the students' behaviour.

Figure 5.1: Steps to personal achievement

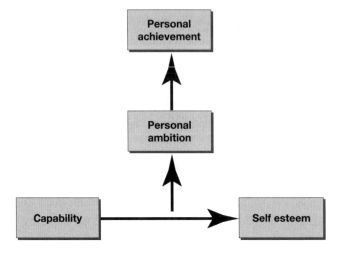

Identity

At the time of publication, the project is still ongoing and planning is under way in the school to make it a permanent part of the school curriculum. The students are starting to realise the enormous power they had been exerting and to understand that they can use their authority in a variety of ways, each of which will have a different consequence. They are starting to see themselves as learners, as people who have choices, and that they can go on exercising those choices for the rest of their lives.

The Middle

The programme was originally designed to last six weeks, though its success meant that the school invited me to design a programme that would last until the end of the academic year. This was then extended again, so that the programme would last until the end of year 11 (the end of compulsory education at 16 years old). The programme was redesigned with a more ambitious agenda. The outline of the programme is described in Figure 5.2.

Figure 5.2: Magic Learning – Social Inclusion Programme

The outline of each session within the programme was always the same. Each session followed this pattern, though what varied was the amount of time spent on each section. Sessions were planned, though always with alternatives and the realisation that what would happen would be unpredictable.

Session Outline

Learning activity introduction – 10 minutes
We are all intrinsically motivated learners. We cannot stop ourselves from solving problems. Our brains work as self-organising mechanisms that create order in our world. In order to engage the students at this level of learning, the sessions began by a simple problem being there for them when they came in. Some were simple activities taken from Feuerstein's work, some from de Bono's CoRT

programme, some from Christmas crackers and some we designed ourselves. Their purpose was to start the students thinking. They proved more irresistible than a smile.

Debunking – open-ended

This session is so important to developing the trust and openness that is essential to the whole programme. It is there to allow the students to get rid of the baggage of the week. The agenda is totally open, though the mediation of the two staff is crucial. Their interventions are never judgemental, which took time for the students to accept. Initially they were waiting for a response, and probably a shock-horror reaction. When they didn't get it they began to raise the stakes of the stories they were telling until they were making them up for our benefit. With still no judgements being made, they gave up and began to use this session much more constructively.

The emphasis within the 'debunk' was always on asking what students wanted and how they might achieve it. 'Why' questions were avoided because they are judgemental. Sometimes the students were reluctant to open up and would say they didn't know how they were going to achieve what they wanted, or didn't know what they wanted at all. Sometimes the students were real in this and sometimes just playing games. Either way they were very skilled game players. Questions were then phrased to presuppose success in order to move the dialogue forward. For example, if a student said they didn't know what they wanted from a particular situation, a dialogue something like the following might take place:

Teacher: "What do you want from this situation?"
Student: "I don't know."
Teacher: "And when you have achieved this thing that you want, what will it be like?"
Student: "It will be better than it is now."
Teacher: "And when it is better than it is now, what will it be like?"

The dialogue would continue, with the student slowly painting the picture of what it was they wanted. Sometimes learning comes in a bright flash with a great bang. This was a slow 'WOW'.

The first pillar of Emotional Intelligence is emotional literacy; understanding how we feel and being able to describe it. Describing emotions is not always best done through words. The students had explored a variety of ways through which they could begin to describe how they felt. They decided that the best way forward was to use animals as a metaphor of their feelings. One of the students made a worksheet and copies for everyone else; the worksheet had pictures of a number of different animals. They began the debunking session by describing which animal they felt like and then explaining *why* they felt like that particular animal at that time and whether or not they were happy with that.

Learning activity 2 – 35 minutes

The first learning activity was usually sedentary, reflective and individual. The debunking sessions had the effect of energising the students and creating a bond between them. In order to build on this, the second learning session was usually kinaesthetic and group-focused.

The activities themselves are neutral in terms of learning. It was not the content but the process that was important. The activities were the vehicle of learning, with the mediation of the staff directing the learning.

Some old favourites were wheeled out. Building the best tower out of newspaper and sticky tape created a lot of energy and a tremendous amount of learning. The students were just told to build the best tower without being told what constituted the best. It was in the debrief that issues were explored about group work, leadership, clarifying the purpose of the task, understanding what we are doing without knowing how others are judging us, and so on. The developing theme was the students taking responsibility for their learning and a developing awareness of their emotional state and its impact on success.

'Making eggs fly' had a certain risk element to it, as it involved a raw egg; the task was to be able to drop an egg from a designated place and have it land without breaking. The students were given an egg, two balloons, a piece of sugar paper, sticky tape and scissors. There were a lot of questions about "Can I do…?" The answer was always the same: "If you want to." Running through this second session was the recurring theme of choice and consequence. You can do whatever you like, *but* you must accept the consequences of your choice.

As the programme developed, the activities become less kinaesthetic and less group focused. The students began to use language that surprised the staff in its complexity and range of vocabulary. Interestingly, they also started to mirror the vocabulary of the staff, asking each other to 'share' a problem or a feeling and beginning to be more positive in the language they used to describe one another.

Debrief – 15 minutes

The debrief would usually start with an opportunity for the students to describe their sense of the experiences they had had during the session. We all have differing views of a shared experience and in order to begin to develop rapport and empathy, understanding this is crucial. It is also critical to learn that it is OK to have differing views of the same experience.

The nature of the mediation in the debrief is crucial to the level of learning and rested heavily on the reflective skills developed by Carl Rogers in the late 1960s and 70s and the Gestalt techniques of Fritz Perls. This approach to mediation is central to the programme and can be easily learnt. It then becomes a very powerful tool in the conventional classroom.

Break – 10 minutes

With a two-hour session there was an expectation by the students that there should be a break. It was useful because it helped their learning. We know that people learn better at the beginning and end of a session, so having more starts and finishes is a real help to learning. This is sometimes called the 'Primacy' and 'Recency' effect. It was also an opportunity for the students to take responsibility to be back on time. Initially they used the break to challenge what they saw as the authority of the staff. When they found that their individual behaviour was not being 'rewarded' by becoming the focus of attention, but that the use of the break was being reviewed in a group context, peer pressure exerted its influence and the break became a more constructive experience.

Learning activity 3 – 35 minutes

In the early stages of the programme this was usually kinaesthetic though often done in pairs or triads rather than the whole group. The debrief was increasingly done by the students themselves. This helped to build trust and break down the factionalism that marked the group at the start of the programme.

As the programme developed, the learning became more focused and the students were able to engage with a fuller range of activities associated with EQ programmes. They were making progress through the levels of learning. They had begun by being very focused on the 'environment' and 'behaviour' of learning. They then were able to progress to activities that engaged them with 'capability' and finally they began to consider issues concerned with 'belief' and 'identity' of learning. They went from the 'When?' and 'What?' of learning to the 'How?' and 'Why?' and finally to the 'Who?' of learning. The students began to reflect on themselves as learners and on the fabulous learning potential and influence they have.

The programme was a success and allowed students who were heading rapidly towards a brick wall to reconsider their present and consider its impact on the future they wanted to build. The level of the success will only be judged through the passage of time, and two hours on a Friday afternoon was always going to limit the achievement that was possible. It was, however, enough for the staff concerned with the programme to be determined to introduce an Emotional Intelligence programme as part of the learning experience for every student in the school from year 7 (11-year-olds) upwards.

A learning session within the programme might look like the following.

Opening the Channels for Learning

Learning activity: An introduction

●　　　●　　　●

●　　　●　　　●

●　　　●　　　●

- Join up the dots using no more than 4 straight lines and without taking your pen off the paper.
- Draw the dots on the board and put out paper and pens. See what happens.
- The answer to the problem is shown below. The problem becomes a great metaphor for the student's thinking. Think outside the dots!

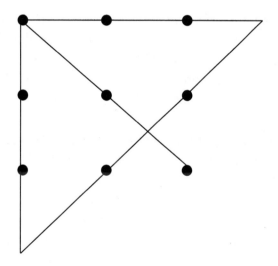

Water water
- A man goes into a pub and asks for a glass of water. The landlord pulls out a shotgun and points it at him and he goes away happy. Why?
- The students can ask any questions they want, but you can answer only 'yes' or 'no'.

Answer: The man had hiccups.

Learning activity 2: Making eggs fly

- Provide the group with:

  A sheet of sugar paper
  A pair of scissors
  2 balloons
  Some sticky tape
  Some string
  An egg

- The task is to be able to drop the egg from a suitable place and have it land without breaking, using *only* the materials given.

Learning activity 3: Lesson for the conflict escalator

Objective:

> *To introduce conflict resolution*
> *To visualise how conflicts escalate and the feelings that build into anger*

1. *Write and perform a brief role play where there will be conflict.*
2. *Thank the actors and draw an escalator on the board or flip chart paper.*
3. *Explain the concept of the escalator.*
4. *What were some of the words or actions that escalated the conflict? List those words as they come to you. List them in chronological order as you go up the escalator.*

Along with each of these words come feelings. What are the feelings that go along with the word 'quick'? Under the first stair, write down the feelings; most likely they will be shock or surprise! Continue on up the escalator.

5. *Explain the concept of baggage. As we travel up an escalator we always have a suitcase with us that holds our baggage. For example it could hold:*

   - *a past relationship with the person*
   - *past experiences with conflict*
   - *feelings about self etc.*

6. *Draw the down side of the escalator.*
7. *Ask the students what it would take to de-escalate the conflict. List the solutions and then write CAPS on each of the steps:*

> *C = Cool Off*
> *A = Agree to work it out*
> *P = Points of view on the problem*
> *S = Solve the problem*

Going up the conflict escalator

- Every behaviour in the conflict is either a step up or a step down the conflict escalator.
- Behaviour that makes the conflict worse will take it another step up the escalator.
- Every step up the conflict escalator has feelings that go with it. As the conflict escalates, so do the feelings.
- No one gets on the escalator empty-handed. They always have a suitcase. That's the baggage they bring to the conflict. Baggage can be filled with:

Past relationship with the person
Current feelings about the person
Past experiences with conflict
Current feelings about conflict
Feelings about self
Mood that day
And more:

_____

_____

The higher you go up the escalator, the harder it is to come down.

William J. Kreidler, 1991

Coming down the conflict escalator

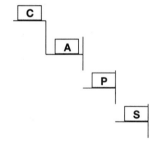

C = Cool off
Deep breaths
Relax muscles
Talk to yourself
Count backwards
Leave

A = Agree to work it out
Don't escalate further
Show willingness – "let's talk it out"

P = POV (points of view) on the problem
Each gives point of view
Use 'I' statements
Use active listening

S = Solve the problem
Brainstorm solutions
Choose a win–win situation
Decide how to implement it

William J. Kreidler, 1991

Chapter Six

Conclusion – The Magic Learning Programme

"The future is not some place we are going but one we are creating. The paths to it are not found but made, the activity of making them changes both the maker and the destination."
John Schaar
Futurist

Developing courses in emotional learning means concentrating on *process* rather than *content*; it is about focusing on *how* things are done in your classroom and providing a vehicle that will take the learning in every subject to new levels of success and allow the students to bridge their learning from the classroom to their lives.

The Magic Learning Programme provides access to Emotional Intelligence for every subject within primary and secondary education. The complete programme is published separately, but the major foundation blocks of the programme are:

- **The What of Emotional Learning.** What will be learnt through each of the levels of learning, and what you will experience in your classroom.
- **The Where and the When of Emotional Learning.** This covers two major issues: where, within the levels of learning, should the programme start and in what sequence should it progress?
- **The How of Emotional Learning.** Developing emotional learning in the classroom is about doing something differently. Like folding your arms the other way around, it will feel strange at first. This section describes the staff development programme that will help staff through the uncomfortable period until it feels natural and wonderful to be helping learning in this way.

The 'When and Where' of Emotional Learning

I have stressed the need to manage change by finding the right point of leverage to achieve the maximum results. Often we find ourselves pushing too hard in the wrong place, for apparently good though misguided reasons.

We often have a good idea about raising standards in school, we are clear about what we want to achieve, but we look for the point of leverage – the point where change can be effected – in the wrong place. We continue to look where the light appears to be brightest, perhaps at the effort the students are putting into their learning. By developing emotional learning we now start to look in a place where we can find the key to raising standards and make the effort students put into their learning give them the results they deserve.

The 'How' of Emotional Learning

Creating the environment for learning, understanding the behaviour of learning, developing the capability and showing students how they can learn to believe in the power of their ability is the basis of the Magic Learning Programme. The first step is that teachers see themselves as learners and as facilitators in the process of learning. This is not a position that all teachers find comfortable. The 'Magic Learning' training allows the participants to successfully see themselves as learners and understand how they can guide others on the same journey.

The 'What' of Emotional Learning

In order to fully develop emotional intelligence through all the levels of learning, a conscious decision has to be taken about when and where the work should be focused. The when and where of developing emotional learning can be summarised in the sequence shown in Figure 6.1. I am not suggesting that you 'do' environment and then move on to 'belief' and so on. You will need to keep your role as 'plate spinner', but the sequence will help you to decide where your initial focus should be.

Figure 6.1: The when and where of developing emotional learning

Creating belief and capability

1. Ambition
   * Making goals the right size
   * Setting goals

2. Self-awareness
   * How I learn
   * How do other people do it?
   * My emotions and learning
   * How well am I doing?

3. Optimism
   * Reframing my experience
   * How optimistic am I?
   * Keeping it in perspective
   * Making it happen – personal efficacy

4. Empathy
   * What I can learn from others
   * How I can learn from others
   * Developing rapport
   * Dealing with conlict

5. Integrity
   * Feeling good about me

Summary – Emotional Intelligence and the Future

The increasing interest in Emotional Intelligence is one of the most exciting developments in education and training in recent years. For too long, the power of emotion has been ignored, and so many children have been unable to reach their potential because their learning needs have gone unrecognised.

There is no simple or straightforward answer to the learning needs of young people today. What is clear is that if we carry on doing what we have always done then the general decline in the quality of experience in our schools for students and teachers will continue. There are many people who are contributing to a crucial debate about the effectiveness of education. There are some very provocative and valuable ideas which have developed our knowledge about learning and how the brain works more than ever before.

As we move into the twenty-first century, Emotional Intelligence must become one of the cornerstones of lifelong learning, helping to create the environment in which we are all able to develop into the fabulous learners we have the potential to be.

If you would like to learn more about the Magic Learning Programme or Emotional Intelligence and its impact on learning, the following contact addresses may prove useful:

Michael Brearley: msbrearley@ntlworld.com
Crown House Publishing: www.crownhouse.co.uk

Bibliography

Branden, Nathaniel (1995). *Six Pillars of Self Esteem: The Definitive Work on Self-Esteem by the Leading Pioneer in the Field*. Bantam.

Claxton, Guy (1998). *Hare Brain, Tortoise Mind: Why Intelligence Increases When You Think Less*. Fourth Estate.

Cooper, Robert & Ayman Sawaf (1998). *Executive EQ: Emotional Intelligence in Business*. Orion.

Covey, Stephen (1999). *The Seven Habits of Highly Effective People: Powerful Lessons in Personal Change*. Simon & Schuster.

Csikszentmihaly, Mihaly (1991). *Flow: The Psychology of Optimal Experience*. Harper Perennial.

de Bono, Edward (1993). *Teach Your Child How to Think*. Penguin.

Dennison, Paul & Gail E. Dennison (1994). *Brain Gym: Teachers Edition Revised*. Edu-Kinesthetics.

Dilts, Robert & Todd Epstein (1995). *Dynamic Learning*. Meta Publications.

Ekman, Paul & Wallace Friesen (1972). *Unmasking the Face*. Englewood Cliffs.

Gardner, Howard (1993). *Frames of Mind: The Theory of Multiple Intelligences*. Fontana Press.

Gelb, Michael J. (1998). *How to Think like Leonardo da Vinci: Seven Steps to Everyday Genius*. HarperCollins.

Goleman, Daniel (1996). *Emotional Intelligence: Why It Can Matter More Than IQ*. Bloomsbury.

Goleman, Daniel (1998). *Working with Emotional Intelligence*. Bloomsbury.

Higgs, M. & V. Dulewicz (1999). *Making Sense of Emotional Intelligence*. NFER Nelson.

Kohn, Alfie (1995). *Punished by Rewards: The Trouble with Gold Stars, Incentive Plans, A's, Praise and Other Bribes*. Houghton Mifflin Company.

Lewkowicz, Adina Bloom (1999). *Teaching Emotional Intelligence: Making Informed Choices*. Skylight.

Perkins, David (1995). *Outsmarting IQ: The Emerging Science of Learnable Intelligence*. Free Press.

Riding, Richard & Stephen Rayner (1998). *Cognitive Styles and Learning Strategies: Understanding Style Differences in Learning and Behaviour*. David Fulton.

Seligman, Martin (1998). *Learned Optimism: How to Change Your Mind and Your Life*. Simon & Schuster.

Simmons, Steve & John C. Simmons Jr. (1997). *Measuring Emotional Intelligence: The Groundbreaking Guide to Applying the Principles of Emotional Intelligence*. Summit.

Smith, Alistair (1998). *Accelerated Learning in Practice*. Network Educational Press.

Smith, Alistair (1996). *Accelerated Learning in the Classroom*. Network Educational Press.

Zohar, Danah & Ian Marshall (1999). *SQ: The Ultimate Intelligence*. Bloomsbury.

Index